MACMILLAN COLOR SERIES

UNIFORMS OF
THE CIVIL WAR

1861—1865

in color

PHILIP J. HAYTHORNTHWAITE

Illustrated by Michael Chappell

'All's quiet along the Potomac tonight
No sound save the rush of the river;
While soft falls the dew on the face of the dead –
The picket's off duty forever.'

Popular song of the Civil War

MACMILLAN PUBLISHING CO., INC.
New York

355.14
H

Copyright © 1975 by Blandford Press Ltd

Macmillan Publishing Co., Inc.
866 Third Avenue, New York, N.Y. 10022

Publication Data
Haythornthwaite, Philip J
Uniforms of the Civil War, 1861–65.
Bibliography: p.
1. United States. Army–Uniforms. 2. Confederate States of America. Army–Uniforms. 3. United States. Navy–Uniforms. 4. United States–History–Civil War, 1861–1865. I. Chappell, Michael. II. Title.
UC483.H39 1976 355.1'4'0973 75-28111
ISBN 0-02-549200-4

First American Edition 1976

Printed in Great Britain

CONTENTS

PREFACE TO THE AMERICAN EDITION

The Civil War was the last conflict in the United States that saw such diverse and colorful uniforms. The Indian Wars of the following period were fought largely by regulars with issue garments, and the Spanish American War, though having a large number of volunteers, saw little diversity in uniforms either. One could say that the Civil War was the last colorful (in the literal sense of the term) conflict in the United States. The text and illustrations in this volume show the romantic flavor of the volunteer participants on both sides in a dramatic way.

The Americans met their requirements for militia service in varying ways from the Colonial period through the Civil War. Many men simply reported for the prescribed drills or musters in whatever garments they had – civilian, military or combinations of both – to fulfill their legal obligations. Others formed companies or smaller units, and held frequent drills, parades, balls and other social events in which they could display their elaborate, distinctive uniforms. Their motivations were both interest in the military and the glamour that was associated with the mystique of military uniforms. In many cases membership in these organizations imparted a social status similar to that of membership in a very exclusive club.

When the call to arms was made in 1861, the volunteers reported for duty wearing clothing that reflected their militia requirements. They wore either civilian clothes or the most exotic of peacetime uniforms. The names of the later groups reflected the same unique *esprit de corps* seen in their choice of military garments. The Zouaves are an example of one exotic uniform style adopted from abroad.

As the war progressed, both sides saw fewer and fewer of the exotic uniforms; however, they never disappeared completely. As certain units distinguished themselves in battle, their unusual uniforms became symbols of their exploits. This was recognized by the United States government when it continued to authorize the manufacture of 'non-regular' uniforms in government depots or by contract, with the proviso that the cost would not exceed that of the regulation issue garments. If the cost was higher, the unit was permitted to have these uniforms made if they would pay the additional cost.

These units were in the minority, since most Northern units found it more practical to adopt the readily accessible issue garments when their original uniforms wore out. In the South the situation was similar, with the additional factors of the shortage of cloth and broken lines of trans-

7

portation through parts of the Confederacy. Diversity grew where the situation required utilization of every available material.

This book is not, nor was it intended to be, the final definitive work on uniforms of the Civil War. It is based upon the standard secondary sources supplemented by primary source material in the form of extant original or republished photographs. For those individuals who want more information on specific units, works in the bibliography – such as individual articles in the *Military Collector & Historian* or similar periodicals – may be consulted. Charles E. Dornbusch's volumes present the histories of specific regiments, along with photographs and descriptions of the various uniforms worn by member organizations at different times prior to, during and subsequent to the Civil War.

There may also be readers who have information that is contradictory to the information in the text or the plates, and in these cases the differences can be resolved by consulting the sources mentioned above. It should be mentioned here that some units, particularly Zouave-type groups, had several uniforms that varied in color and trim at various stages. This point, unfortunately, has been the basis of many bitter arguments in which both parties are actually correct but the exact date of the change, the real crux of the argument, was never determined.

It is interesting to note that this American conflict is still of such wide-ranging interest that a foreign author found it desirable to devote time and effort to an entire book on uniforms of the period. This reflects the growth and wide geographical expansion of interest in the Civil War. The reader will note that this book was published in Great Britain for a British audience. In a few instances the terminology may be somewhat confusing to an American reader. The term *rank bar*, for instance, is termed a 'shoulder strap' in the official U.S Army Regulations and includes both the strap, worn parallel and next to the shoulder seam, and the insignia of rank device for all grades of officers, not just the bar device used by the first lieutenant. The official term 'binding' is used for the material of the chevrons in the regulations for both the North and South, and the term 'braid' refers to the Confederate officer's sleeve rank trim, while in Great Britain the term *lace* is more commonly used to refer to both binding and 'braid'. In those cases where the terminology is ambiguous to American readers, it is suggested that they consult the actual regulations (see bibliography). These, together with the illustrations, should make any confusing points clear.

In the case of volunteer organizations, problems in terminology can

8

be resolved by consulting the same type of sources for further details on specific units. For instance, the term 'stocking cap' would indicate to the American a soft knit item, as opposed to the stiff fez which is our own popular term for the Zouave-type headgear. Again, careful examination of the illustrations should make the identification of the object clear. The terms 'drafted' and 'regimented' are also used in the British sense. The use of the various conscription acts by both North and South can be clarified by checking cited sources.

One point that should be noted is the use of the dark blue versus the sky blue trousers. The most commonly consulted Union Army uniform reference, the *Army Regulations of 1861*, call for dark blue trousers for all ranks. *The Revised Army Regulations of 1863* carry the same information, but *General Orders No. 8, Headquarters of the Army*, dated 16 December, 1861, direct that regimental officers and enlisted men were to have trousers of 'sky-blue' mixture. The fact that this order was overlooked in the 1863 revision of the *Regulations* has caused much confusion.

For the convenience of the beginner in this field, a useful historical introduction has been included. While most of this information may be known to the advanced scholar, it is convenient to have all the background information in one compact volume.

In conclusion, I feel that this book will be of interest and benefit to students of uniforms of the Civil War, and to all persons interested in military history. In one volume, many delightful illustrations of uniforms of the period are combined with useful background information.

Donald E. Kloster
Uniform Specialist
Washington, D.C.

Erratum. Pl. 59, Infantry in 'Butternut': the blanket referred to in the text (page 180) is a woven blanket and not a gum blanket.

HISTORICAL INTRODUCTION

The Civil War 1861–65

In so a short a survey, there is little room for an enumeration of the causes of the most devastating war ever waged in America. Very briefly, the United States in the late 1850's was sharply divided. The northern states, in particular those on the eastern seaboard, were democratic and forward-thinking, with large numbers of European immigrants, basing their economy upon industry and (in the western states) agriculture. The southern states, on the other hand, based their economy upon the growing of cotton, but by the late 1850's were conscious of gradually becoming the 'poor relations' of the north.

With these two different economies, and with major differences in politics and social ways, the North and the South began to clash on major issues. A significant bone of contention was the question of slavery: forbidden in the north, yet part of the very nature of the south. In the northern states there was a growing anti-slavery movement, which erupted into violence in 1859 when John Brown, a religious fanatic, seized the Armoury at Harper's Ferry to use as a base for a 'religious crusade' to free the slaves in the south. After a sharp fight with U.S. Marines under Colonel Robert E. Lee, Brown was captured and hanged for treason.

Brown's death aroused widespread indignation among the anti-slavery factions and it was obvious that the coming Presidential election would concentrate upon the slavery question, in particular how it affected the new territories on the fringe of the westward expansion of 'civilisation'. When the Republican candidate, Abraham Lincoln, was elected President, the southern states saw only one way to keep slavery and thereby preserve their agricultural economy: secession from the Union and the establishment of their own, independent nation. On 20 December 1860 the legislature of South Carolina declared the state an independent commonwealth, no longer a member of the Union.

Such a decision was anathema to nothern politicians, who regarded the Union as an indivisible entity, but South Carolina was soon joined by Mississippi, Florida, Alabama, Georgia, Louisiana and Texas, who elected their own government and appointed Jefferson Davies as President of the Confederate States of America (9 February 1861).

It was obvious to all that the north would not take the secession of so large a part of the country without a word, so two days after Lincoln's inauguration, President Davis called for 100,000 one-year volunteers: by mid-April 1861 the Confederacy had 35,000 men under arms, a force twice as big as the small Federal army.

Lincoln made an attempt to supply the U.S. garrison at Fort Sumter in Charleston Harbour, which precipitated a bombardment by South Carolinan forces under General Beauregard. On 14 April Fort Sumter capitulated, and the following day Lincoln called for 75,000 volunteers to suppress the insurrection. Virginia – still part of the Union – claimed this call was an act of war upon the seceded states, and seceded herself, followed by Arkansas, Tennessee and North Carolina; by 20 May eleven states were in armed, open rebellion; Kentucky declared neutrality on 24 May. In retaliation, Lincoln proclaimed a blockade of southern ports.

The two 'countries'

On paper, the twenty-two northern states had an overwhelming advantage: their population was 22,000,000 (as against 5,500,000 whites in the South); the North had both agriculture and heavy industry, while the Confederacy depended upon export of its cotton, sugar and tobacco in exchange for the war materials it was largely unable to manufacture for itself. Lincoln's blockade exerted a stranglehold from which the South could never free itself, causing shortages of weapons and ammunition which increased steadily as the war progressed.

The Confederate 'army' consisted solely of new recruits and local militia and volunteer companies, poorly-trained and equipped, reinforced by the professional élite of 313 officers who had left the U.S. Army upon the secession of their native states; only twenty-six other ranks deserted to the Confederacy. In the early months of the war, the North also had to rely upon their militia companies, as the regular army was small and spread along the western frontier and the eastern coast. When the war broke out, the Union had only four warships in commission in northern waters, though the Confederacy had no ships at all, only a quantity of 'seceded' officers, and indeed little provision for building any ships, the major shipyards all being in the North.

The greatest tragedy of the war was the fact that it was, truly, a 'civil' war – the number of divided families was quite staggering. Three cases show how America was 'a nation divided': President Lincoln's wife had a brother, three half-brothers, and three brothers-in-law in the Confederate Army; at Gettysburg, the Union 7th West Virginia (commanded by Lieutenant-Colonel Lockwood) attacked the Confederate 7th Virginia. One of the Confederate officers wounded and captured was Colonel Lockwood's nephew. But the tragedy which overtook the entire nation is best demonstrated by the case of Captain Franklin Buchanan, commander of the *C.S.S. Virginia*, which sank the *U.S.S. Congress* in March 1862. Buchanan's brother was Paymaster of the *Congress*, killed when the ship sank. Such tragic events were repeated throughout the war; at Shiloh a young Kentuckian was seen to point at the enemy line and call to his brother at his side: 'Hold on Bill, don't shoot any more! There's father!'

The opening battles

On 20 April 1861, Virginian militia captured the Norfolk Navy Yard, an important gain for the Confederacy, together with the steam-frigate *Merrimack* and large quantities of heavy armaments. In May, Washington (the Federal capital) was briefly menaced, and at Boonville (1 June) a Confederate threat to St. Louis was defeated. Throughout the month there was skirmishing in West Virginia.

The first main sphere of operations was around the two capitals, Washington and Richmond, Virginia, where the Confederate government was installed. General McDowell with 38,000 Union troops (less than 2,000 regulars among them) moved out on 19 July to attack Beauregard, who had 20,000 Confederates near Centerville, Virginia. Unaware that Confederate General Joseph Johnston had arrived with a 12,000 reinforcement, McDowell attacked at the First Battle of Bull Run with a plan too complicated for his untrained militia. His assault was stopped by General Thomas J. Jackson's Virginian brigade, Jackson being described as 'standing like a stone wall', impervious to Union attacks, thus earning him his famous sobriquet, 'Stonewall'. As Johnston's reinforcements came up by rail (an important innovation in the history of warfare), McDowell's volunteers were outflanked and fled in panic. The few regulars covered the retreat of the militia, and President Davis forbade any pursuit, which might have led to the capture of the Federal capital had it been allowed.

The Union replaced McDowell with General McClellan, who set about reorganising and training what was to become the 'Army of the Potomac', so that the débâcle of First Bull Run should not be repeated. On 10 August 1861 Union General Lyon stopped a Confederate advance on Missouri at Wilson's Creek, though at the cost of his own life. In mid-September, General Robert E. Lee (who had captured John Brown), now in the Army of the Confederacy, was repulsed by Union troops at Cheat Mountain in an attempt to recover West Virginia. Prior to his personal secession, Lee had been offered command of the Union forces by Lincoln; he declined and joined the Confederacy. On 21 October at Ball's Bluff a small Union force was annihilated, but on 7 November Union General Ulysses S. Grant made a hit-and-run attack on Belmont, relieving Confederate pressure on Missouri. 1861 ended without further military action; McClellan was appointed Union General-in-Chief in place of the ancient hero, Winfield Scott, retired because of his advanced age; an unfortunate decision on the part of the Union as Scott (a Southerner by birth) was still the most capable military brain in the country despite his years.

The naval actions of 1861 were confined to the Northern blockade of Southern ports, including the establishment of two Union bases on the Confederate coast, at Hatteras Inlet and Port Royal. The only Confederate 'naval' ships in existence were a few 'privateers', converted merchantmen which prowled the coast looking for easy 'kills'.

The first year of the war ended in stalemate; both sides were arming for the first serious campaigning, the Confederacy having to rely to a great extent upon imported war materials brought from Europe by 'blockade runners'. The only major battle – First Bull Run – had shown the amateurism of both sides; though a Confederate victory, their failure to pursue the broken Union army was a major blunder.

War in the East, 1862

McClellan, with 180,000 men near Washington, was nervous of advancing on Johnston's 50,000 Confederates opposing him, until goaded into action by Lincoln personally; McClellan thereupon resolved upon a circuitous advance on Richmond.

On 8 March the *C.S.S. Virginia* – the old *Merrimack* converted into a strong 'ironclad' warship, proof against most naval artillery, sailed out of Norfolk towards the Union blockading squadron. In a spectacular

13

battle, the *Virginia* rammed and sank the *U.S.S. Cumberland*, sank the *U.S.S. Congress*, and forced the *U.S.S. Minnesota* aground. Returning undamaged to Norfolk, the *Virginia* intended to defeat the remaining three Union ships the following day. But to counter the threat of the 'invincible' Confederate warship, the U.S. Navy rushed the *U.S.S. Monitor* to the scene, a small, revolutionary, armoured warship described as resembling 'a cheese-box on a raft', armed with only two guns in its revolving turret. Next day the two armoured ships battered away at each other without effect until the *Virginia* withdrew, leaving the *Monitor* in control of Hampton Roads. This inconclusive action revolutionised naval warfare by proving wooden ships obsolete.

Lincoln, uncertain of McClellan's capabilities, assumed overall command personally, an understandable move but one which proved disastrous. Afraid of an attack on Washington by 'Stonewall' Jackson's small force (4,300), Lincoln detached part of McClellan's army to cover the capital. Jackson attacked this covering force at Kernstown (23 March) and though repulsed threw Lincoln into such a panic over fears for the safety of Washington that he detached even more of McClellan's force. Robert E. Lee, realising Lincoln's sensitivity over the capital, advised President Davis to reinforce Jackson, who could then divert even more Union troops.

As the Valley Campaign opened, Jackson vigorously began his task of keeping the Union forces occupied, defeating Federal forces at McDowell (8 May), Front Royal (23 May) and the First Battle of Winchester (25 May). Lincoln's reaction was as expected: he drew more men from McClellan's planned offensive; Jackson skilfully evaded converging Union forces, beating them at Cross Keys (8 June) and Port Republic (9 June). In his brilliant little campaign, Jackson's 18,000 men had tied up 70,000 Federal troops, captured vast quantities of valuable arms, cannon and stores, and changed the entire Union plan of campaign.

The Peninsula Campaign

McClellan, with a much-depleted force, moved up the Peninsula between the York and James Rivers towards Richmond. Faced with a ten-mile line of entrenchments manned by dummy guns, the nervous McClellan requested siege artillery and slowly began to bombard the fortified line. Johnston's Confederates had retired two days before the

14

bombardment commenced! As McClellan moved ponderously forward, he was held up at Williamsburg by General Longstreet's Confederate rearguard, then pressed on within sight of Richmond. Dividing his force in half, McClellan's left was fallen upon by Johnston at Seven Pines (1 June 1862), but poor co-ordination in the Confederate attacks led to their repulse when McClellan hurried up reinforcements. With Johnston severely wounded, the Confederate government reorganised their forces in the area as the Army of Northern Virginia, with General R. E. Lee in command.

Lee then set about repelling the threat to Richmond; General J. E. B. Stuart led a cavalry raid to the Federal rear, destroying much of McClellan's stores, but the first Confederate attack which opened the Seven Days' Battles was repulsed by the Union at Mechanicsville (26 June). Next day, Lee attacked General Porter's Union corps, which fell back in good order. As Lee followed, McClellan was unable to see that Richmond was open for capture, and continued to withdraw. On 29–30 June more Confederate attacks were repulsed, and at Malvern Hill (1 July) Lee was decisively thrown back by Porter. Incredibly, McClellan ordered further withdrawal. In the Seven Days' Battles, the Confederacy had lost more men (about 20,000 to the Union 15,000), and had been beaten everywhere except at Gaines' Mill; but strategically, McClellan's retreat had brought about a Confederate success.

Second Bull Run Campaign

Lincoln, well aware of the need for a change in command and organisation, appointed General Pope to command the Union Army of Virginia, General Halleck as General-in-Chief, and ordered the Army of the Potomac back to Washington. On 9 August, Union General Banks attacked 'Stonewall' Jackson at Cedar Mountain, but was driven back; Jackson also withdrew. Lee, learning that McClellan was coming to join Pope (which would mean that the Confederate army would be outnumbered by three to one), decided to defeat Pope before McClellan arrived.

Jackson marched fifty-four miles in two days, placed himself behind Pope, and captured the Union general's supply depot. Again acting as a decoy, Jackson revealed his position deliberately by an attack at Groveton, leading the enraged Pope on to a prepared defensive position at the old Bull Run battlefield. The decoy worked: Pope threw himself at Jackson, only to find himself taken in the flank by Lee with Longstreet's Confederate corps (30 August). Decisively beaten, Pope withdrew towards Washington, the Confederate pursuit being checked by Union reinforcements under General Kearny at Chantilly (31 August), where Kearny was killed.

Antietam Campaign

Davis was anxious for a substantial Confederate victory, which might win the recognition – and perhaps assistance – of Britain and France. Lee was therefore ordered to carry the war into the North. Splitting his army (55,000 strong), Lee began his advance, though put himself at the mercy of McClellan, coming up with the Army of the Potomac. (Pope had been transferred and his surviving units incorporated in McClellan's army.) Vacillating as ever, McClellan marched only ten miles in two days, allowing Lee time to concentrate his divided command at Sharpsburg, delaying McClellan further by a covering action at South Mountain (14 September). McClellan still refused to attack, losing a golden opportunity of destroying Lee piecemeal, until Lee and Jackson (having captured the Union garrison of Harper's Ferry) prepared a defensive position along Antietam creek.

On 17 September – three days too late – McClellan decided to attack. In an all-out assault on Lee's position, the Union forces achieved early successes, General Burnside's Union corps storming a bridge over the creek. With Lee on the brink of defeat, McClellan refused to commit his 20,000 reserves to deliver the *coup de grâce*; Lee counterattacked and Burnside was flung back across the creek. In the bloodiest single day of the war, Lee had turned the brink of defeat into victory, assisted by McClellan's incompetence. However, having lost 13,700 to the Union 12,400, Lee's invasion was brought to an end; though a tactical Confederate victory, Antietam was strategically a Union success.

This 'victory' for the Union gave Lincoln the chance to issue his Emancipation Proclamation. Taking effect from 1 January 1863, this proclamation marked a dramatic change in the war's focus: no longer a war to preserve the Union, but now a crusade to free the slaves in those states still in rebellion. Giving the Union cause a high moral tone, the Emancipation Proclamation strengthened the resolve of the

Confederacy to resist as fiercely as possible, since the consequence of the enforcement of the proclamation in the south would not only mean economic disaster, but would also bring about a fundamental change in the social fabric of the area.

Fredericksburg Campaign

McClellan refused to follow Lee's withdrawal until ordered to do so by Lincoln; he then advanced so slowly that he was relieved of command and Burnside appointed in his place. Intending to attack Richmond via Fredericksburg, Burnside allowed Lee to prepare a defensive position on the heights above the town; when he did attack, Burnside found an impregnable position facing him, yet poured regiment after regiment into suicidal attacks (13 December). The day ended with 12,500 Union troops mown down without a chance; Burnside wanted to attack again next day, but fortunately for his army he was dissuaded from so doing by his corps commanders. 1862 had ended in the eastern sphere of operations with another Union débâcle.

The War in the West, 1862 – West of the Mississippi

Little of strategic importance occurred west of the Mississippi in 1862; in March, a Confederate attack was beaten off near Fayetteville, Arkansas, at the Battle of Pea Ridge. In February, a small Confederate force attempting to invade California defeated a Union detachment at Valverde, New Mexico, capturing Albuquerque and Santa Fe, but was itself defeated at Peralta on 15 April, and retired to Texas. In December a Confederate attempt to occupy northern Arkansas was defeated by a Union force at Prairie Grove.

The War in the West, 1862 – East of the Mississippi

Confederate fortunes in this sphere began inauspiciously when an advance in eastern Kentucky was decisively repulsed by a Union force at Mill Springs (19–20 January). Between February and April, General U. S. Grant co-ordinated a combined army and gunboat attack up the Tennessee River, capturing Forts Henry and Donelson, and then moved to occupy Nashville. In an attempt to restore fast-fading Confederate hopes of holding the area, General Albert Johnston fell upon Grant's bivouacs at Shiloh on 6 April, the surprise almost winning the day; Grant somehow gathered enough men to counter-attack (assisted by the fire of two gunboats), and the Union position was temporarily restored when Johnston was killed leading a charge. Next day, Grant received reinforcement and attacked immediately; the new Confederate commander, Beauregard, wisely decided to with-draw, with the loss of 10,600 men; Grant had lost 13,000. Grant was much criticised for allowing himself to be surprised, but Lincoln refused to replace him: 'I can't spare this man. He fights!'

In May, Halleck took command of Grant's army, but left when appointed General-in-Chief in July, turning the western command over to Generals Grant and Buell. In September, Grant beat off a renewed Confederate attack at Iuka, but the Confederates were allowed to escape by the errors of Union General Rosecrans; in early October Grant's plans for trapping the Confederates at Corinth again fell foul of Rosecrans' laxity.

Meanwhile, Buell's wing of the western army found itself opposed by Confederate General Bragg, a thoroughly incompetent commander. Defeating a small Federal detachment at Richmond, Kentucky (30 August), Bragg and Buell came face to face at Perryville (8 October). After a Union attack was turned back, Bragg for some reason decided to withdraw, and Buell, equally negligent, failed to pursue him.

Disgusted by Buell's apparent lack of effort, Lincoln replaced him with Rosecrans, who followed his predecessor in avoiding action, as did Bragg. Only Confederate cavalry generals Forrest and Morgan were active, raiding Union positions and destroying supplies. Throughout the war, the cavalry was the Confederacy's best arm, being drawn from the hereditary horsemen of the south; only in the later stages did the Union cavalry ever approach the excellence of the 'natural horsemen' of the southern states.

Berated by their respective governments, both Buell and Bragg decided to attack the enemy's right flank; Bragg attacked first at Stones River (31 December 1862) and so mishandled his reserve that he threw away the chance of a complete victory; Buell managed to patch together a defensive line which turned back a second Con-federate assault, and Bragg withdrew. Tactically drawn, with casualties about equal (Buell 12,906, Bragg 11,740), the Battle of Stones River was a strategic success for the Union, though Rosecrans (the senior commander) deserved little credit for it.

During 1862, Union forces had been advancing down the Mississippi, engaged by Confederate gunboats at Plum Point (9 May), until all but one of the Confederate fleet was sunk at the Battle of Memphis (6 June). From the other direction, Union Admiral Farragut sank nine Confederate gunboats at the Battle of New Orleans (24 April), captured the city and established a Union stronghold there, and moved upriver to link up with the other Union vessels, imposing a river blockade upon Vicksburg. On land, Grant and General William T. Sherman also converged on Vicksburg, while General Banks moved up from New Orleans. Union plans for a combined assault on the town came to a temporary end, however, when Sherman attacked a Confederate position at Chickasaw Bluffs, just north of Vicksburg; after three days of fighting (27–29 December) Sherman withdrew with 1,776 casualties, leaving the Confederates safely in possession of their entrenchments, with only 207 casualties.

At the end of 1862, therefore, though Grant was still in a powerful position, the Confederacy was by no means downhearted; Mississippi from Vicksburg to Baton Rouge was safely defended, and the decisive victory at Fredericksburg had raised Confederate hopes in the eastern sphere. 1863 was to prove somewhat different.

War in the East, 1863

Despite orders to halt, Burnside tried to cross the Rappahannock; bogged down by muddy roads, the Union offensive became a farce, and Burnside was replaced in command of the Army of the Potomac by General Joseph 'Fighting Joe' Hooker; Hooker brought his private habits with him, so that his headquarters became 'a combination of bar-room and brothel'; even Lincoln thought him better fitted for running a tavern than an army, but anyone seemed preferable to poor Burnside.

Hooker planned a two-pronged attack on Lee's ill-supplied Army of Northern Virginia, sending General Sedgwick to attack the Confederates at Fredericksburg, while Hooker himself would assault Lee's left. Leaving General Early to contain Sedgwick, Lee met Hooker's advance at Chancellorsville (1 May). Despite his overwhelming strength, Hooker went onto the defensive and allowed 'Stonewall'

Jackson to smash the Union right wing (2 May). On 3 May Lee pressed forward against increasing Federal resistance, until he received news that Sedgwick had overcome Early's small detachment at Fredericksburg. Despite the worsening Confederate situation, Hooker declined to advance, allowing Lee to turn upon Sedgwick and defeat him at Salem Church (4 May). Hooker pulled back across the Rappahannock River, having lost 16,792 men. Lee had won a tremendous tactical victory, at a cost of 12,754 casualties, but had lost one man the Confederacy could not spare: 'Stonewall' Jackson, perhaps the most outstanding general of the war, had been fired on by his own troops in mistake, and died from his wounds on 10 May; it was a grievous blow for Southern hopes.

Gettysburg Campaign

Lee determined to maintain the initiative and moved over to the Shenandoah Valley; on 9 June there occurred the largest cavalry battle of the war at Brandy Station, when Federal General Pleasanton surprised 'Jeb' Stuart's cavalry corps. It was a drawn action, Pleasanton losing 900 men to Stuart's 500. Union setbacks continued when on 13-14 June the Federal force in the lower Shenandoah was smashed at the Second Battle of Winchester.

As Lee advanced over the Potomac and into Pennsylvania, Hooker's 115,000 men followed the Confederates northwards. Hooker's plan for a two-pronged attack was overruled by Halleck (remembering what had happened to Hooker at Chancellorsville), and Hooker resigned his command. General George Meade was appointed in his stead, the Army of the Potomac's fifth commander in ten months. Lee, though deprived of Stuart's cavalry by the latter raiding in Maryland, concentrated to meet the Federal army. On 30 June 1863 a Confederate brigade heading towards Gettysburg and the store of boots it was reputed to contain, ran into a Union cavalry force, and so began the greatest battle ever fought in North America.

On 1 July heavy fighting took place between the vanguards of both armies, Union General Reynolds being killed as he led his corps into action. As the Union forces organised a defensive line based upon Cemetery Ridge, Cemetery Hill, Culp's Hill, Round Top and Little Round Top hills, the renewed Confederate attack drove the Federals back onto their hill-line. As more of Meade's troops came up, the first day's fighting ended with the Confederates very much in command.

On 2 July Lee renewed his attacks on the strong, now entrenched Union position. Ignoring Longstreet's advice, Lee threw his divisions in with little co-ordination in the late afternoon; attacks on the Round Top–Little Round Top area were repulsed, and at the other end of the Union defence-line the Confederate advance broke down entirely in the face of heavy fire. The advantage gained by the Confederacy on the first day had been wiped out by these haphazard attacks on the Union flanks.

Despite Longstreet's vehement objections, Lee (now reinforced) determined to attack again on 3 July. The first Confederate attack on Meade's position – on the right flank established on Culp's Hill – was beaten back with severe losses to both sides. Having attacked both flanks, Lee decided to hit the Union centre with ten brigades, including those of General Pickett. At 1.45 p.m. the Confederate force rolled forward in the face of severe fire; they penetrated far enough to engage the Federals in hand-to-hand fighting in what has become known as 'Pickett's charge', but the contest could never have been in doubt. As the Confederates retired, shattered, elements of the Union line counter-attacked and Longstreet rallied his men to form their own ragged defence-line. The expected general advance by Meade never material-ised, and Lee began his retreat on the following afternoon (4 July). The waggon-train evacuating the Confederate wounded was seventeen miles long.

A minor success by Stuart's cavalry (which arrived on 2 July) and a deluge of rain delayed Meade's pursuit and Lee escaped. The Con-federate invasion of the north had been thrown back in the action which has been seen as the turning-point of the war. In all, 88,289 Federals and 75,000 Confederates were engaged at Gettysburg; total losses were a staggering 23,049 and 28,063 respectively, a fearful toll. Whole units were shattered: the Union Iron Brigade was destroyed as an effective force, while the 1st Minnesota suffered an incredible 82 per cent casualties in a fifteen-minute charge in Trostle Woods. The 26th North Carolina went into the action over 800 strong; it had 98 effectives at the end of the third day.

Meade failed to follow up his success; a new advance by Lee was checked at Bristoe Station (14 October), and at the end of November Meade himself was repulsed at Mine Run. The war in the east in 1863 ended with neither side having recovered from the climactic and appalling battle of Gettysburg.

As the year opened, Grant determined to press on towards Vicksburg. Sporadic naval actions took place on the river, Farragut steaming up-river to assist. Diverting the Confederate army of General Pemberton defending Vicksburg by skilful cavalry raids, Grant pushed back a Confederate reinforcement attempting to reach the town at Jackson (14 May), and drove Pemberton into Vicksburg itself. Grant's achievement was quite incredible – in nineteen days he had marched 200 miles, living off the land, and defeated a numerically superior enemy in no less than five separate actions; this campaign, taking its name from the Big Black River, has been called the most brilliant ever waged on American soil.

Investing Vicksburg, Grant soon starved the garrison into surrender. Pemberton capitulated on 4 July, and on the same day a Confederate attack on Helena, Arkansas, was repulsed. As Lincoln said, the Mississippi now 'flowed unvexed' to the sea; the Confederacy had been split in two.

While Grant campaigned around Vicksburg, Rosecrans was finally shaken out of six months' inactivity by Halleck's threats to replace him, and moved on Bragg's Confederate army. Falling back on Chattanooga, Bragg was forced to abandon the town as Burnside – now in command of the Union Army of the Ohio – came up behind him. As Rosecrans followed, President Davis rushed Longstreet's corps from the Army of Northern Virginia to reinforce Bragg. With Rosecrans' army strung out on line of march, Bragg attacked at Chickamauga on 19 September, hampered by densely wooded terrain. Attempting to change his formation on the following day, Rosecrans opened a gap in his line through which Longstreet plunged; only the left wing of the Union army, commanded by General G. H. Thomas, 'The Rock of Chickamauga', escaped destruction.

Bragg, indecisive as ever, allowed Rosecrans to withdraw to Chattanooga, to which the Confederate army laid siege. Cut off from reinforcement, Rosecrans faced starvation, but Grant (placed in command of all Union forces in the west by Lincoln on 17 October) broke through the Confederate cordon and relieved Chattanooga. Bragg entrenched his army outside the town on Lookout Mountain and Missionary Ridge, and, so confident of the impregnability of his fortifications, sent Longstreet to besiege Burnside in Knoxville, leaving only 40,000 to defend the entrenched position.

Reinforced by General Sherman to 61,000, Grant attacked Lookout Mountain on 24 November. A combined assault of Sherman and Hooker's corps carried the position, though Sherman's column was repulsed from Missionary Ridge. Much to Bragg's horror, Grant attacked Missionary Ridge on the following day; Bragg's troops, finding their 'impregnable' positions anything but, panicked and fled. Sherman was detached to relieve Knoxville, and arrived to find the siege already lifted. With Tennessee cleared of Confederate troops, the Southern heartland lay open.

Naval Operations, 1863

With the Federal blockade slowly strangling the south's supply-lines with Europe, the ports of Wilmington, North Carolina and Charleston were the main haven for blockade-runners. Repeated Union attacks on Charleston harbour finally resulted in the capture of Fort Wagner on 6 September, but no further foothold could be gained by the Federals. On 5 October came another innovation: a submarine attack by the C.S.S. David, which severely damaged the U.S.S. New Ironsides with an exploding torpedo.

Confederate naval activity was otherwise restricted to the ravages on Union shipping of two British-built privateers, the C.S.S. Alabama and the C.S.S. Florida, though the career of the latter was brought to an untimely end when she was captured in Bahia harbour by the U.S.S. Wachusett, in complete disregard for Brazilian neutrality. The Alabama, however, continued to wreak havoc on the high seas.

War in the East, 1864

Ulysses S. Grant was appointed Federal General-in-Chief in March 1864. The tide of war was already turning against the Confederacy, and Grant planned to end the contest quickly: he would keep Lee's Army of Northern Virginia occupied, while Sherman from the West penetrated into the deep south. Lincoln realised that he had found the leader whom he had sought for so long, and told Grant: 'The particulars of your plan I neither know or seek to know . . . I wish not to obtrude any constraints or restraints upon you.' By forbidding further prisoner-exchanges, Grant struck a severe blow at the Confederate manpower situation.

23

1864 began, however, with two Confederate successes: a Union descent upon Florida was repulsed at the Battle of Olustee (20 February), and a Federal raid on Richmond by General Kilpatrick and 4,500 cavalry ended in disaster.

Grant planned to take personal command of Meade's Army of the Potomac, leaving the administrative duties of General-in-Chief to Halleck in Washington. His intention was to cut off Lee from Richmond, protecting his own line of communication based upon the Virginian ports with the Union navy. Two lesser forces would hopefully prevent Lee's reinforcement.

As soon as Grant moved, Lee opposed him in the 140-square-mile Wilderness, an almost-impenetrable tangle of brush and thicket. On 5 May the fighting was a confused, uncontrollable jumble of small units, and on 6 May Grant attacked in force, meeting strong counter-attacks. The third day was spent by both armies trying to extinguish forest-fires started by the battle, and attempting to rescue wounded from the flames.

Moving round Lee's right, Grant's sporadic fighting from 8 May to 12 May gave Lee the opportunity to form his line into an immense 'V', with the apex – the 'Bloody Angle' – pointing north. Meanwhile, Sheridan's Federal cavalry raided towards Richmond. Sheridan's 10,000 met 'Jeb' Stuart's 4,500 Confederate cavalry on 11 May at Yellow Tavern; heavily outnumbered, Stuart was killed and his force broken, a tremendous blow to the South.

Lee repelled an attack on his position at Spotsylvania on 12 May, whereupon Grant moved off and again tried to outflank him. Lee however, in a brilliant piece of defensive warfare, opposed Grant at North Anna (23 May) and Haw's Shop (28 May), which forced Grant into an all-out frontal attack on entrenched Confederate positions at Cold Harbor. Losing 7,000 men in less than an hour, Grant withdrew, having lost 13,000 from 3–12 June, against Lee's loss of only 3,000.

The two smaller Union forces working in conjunction with Grant, those of Generals Butler and Sigel, were also thrown back at the battles of Drewry's Bluff and New Market respectively (15 May). Unshaken, Grant sent Sheridan's cavalry on a diversionary raid (which was repelled at Trevilian Station on 11–12 June), while Grant at last succeeded in fooling Lee, slipping past, crossing the James River on a pontoon-bridge, and sending Butler to attack Petersburg. Butler failed miserably and by the time Grant arrived and renewed the attack, Petersburg had been garrisoned by Lee to withstand a siege.

In July, General Early's Confederates almost caused a major upset in the war, invading Maryland, routing a Union force on the Monocacy River (9 July) and threatening Washington. The capture of the capital was averted at the last minute by reinforcements sent by Grant, which stopped Early in the very outskirts of the capital. Early retired, then lunged forward again and destroyed the Union Army of West Virginia at Kernstown and Winchester (24–25 July). Grant placed Sheridan in command of the Washington defence forces with orders to secure the capital's safety by devastating Virginia, 'so that crows flying over it . . . will have to carry their own provender'.

Sheridan turned back the Confederates at the Third Battle of Winchester (19 September) and heavily defeated Early at Fisher's Hill (22 September), then moved down the Shenandoah Valley turning it into a 'vale of desolation'. Having completed his task (despite harassment by Confederate guerrillas), Sheridan left his army at Cedar Creek just before Early fell upon it (19 October). The Union VIII Corps stampeded (and was only rallied two days later); but Sheridan returned, reformed the remainder of his army, counter-attacked, and beat off the assault. The defeat ended serious Confederate resistance in the Shenandoah Valley, though Early was not finally overcome until the Battle of Waynesboro in March 1865.

Petersburg, Phase One

Petersburg and the Confederate capital, Richmond, formed one large defensive network; the capture of one or the other would strike the final nail into the Confederate coffin. Grant therefore began a slow encirclement of the Petersburg–Richmond area, to cut off Lee from his sources of supply.

On 22–23 June 1864 a Union probing advance was thrown back; on 30 July, a Union mining operation culminated with the explosion of four tons of gunpowder under the Petersburg defence system. Burnside charged his IX Corps through the gap, but, in a tragic re-enactment of his disaster at Fredericksburg, Burnside's men were cut to pieces by the Confederate defenders. Yet another setback for Grant came when six days of assaulting another sector of the defences, Deep Bottom Run, cost him 2,900 casualties without denting the Confederate position (14–20 August).

On 18–21 August Grant cut the Confederate supply-line of the Weldon Railroad by the Battle of Globe Tavern, though at fearful cost to the Union detachments involved. A Confederate attempt to reopen the railway was beaten back at Ream's Station three days later. On 29–30 September, Fort Harrison on the Richmond sector of the defence-line was captured along with Chaffin's Bluff, and the encirclement inched farther on the 30th when Peeble's Farm was taken. As winter closed in, Grant attempted to cut the last rail link, the Southside Railroad, but was beaten off (27–28 October), and both sides settled down for the winter, the Confederates to a decidedly uncomfortable and hungry one.

War in the West, 1864

The first operations in the west in 1864 were upon Halleck's orders (before Grant was appointed to overall command): the Red River expedition, a combined military and naval (by river gunboats) invasion of Texas, intended primarily to discourage any French intervention on behalf of the Confederacy via their army of occupation currently controlling Mexico. Union General Banks was ambushed at Sabine Cross Roads (8 April), fought a delaying action at Pleasant Hill (9 April), and escaped, the expedition in ruins.

Confederate operations west of the Mississippi were ended when a Confederate force under General Price invaded Missouri; despite successes at Lexington (10 October) and Independence (22 October), Price was defeated and driven back into Arkansas on 23 October at the Battle of Westport.

In northern Mississippi, General Forrest's handful of Confederates enjoyed considerable success against greatly superior Union forces; at the Battle of Oklona (22 February) a Union force of between two and three times Forrest's strength was routed. Forrest then raided into Kentucky, capturing Fort Pillow (12 April) where it was alleged some of his men massacred Union coloured troops after their surrender. On 10 June Forrest routed a much superior Union force at Brice's Cross Roads, but received his first setback at Tupelo (14–15 July). In August, however, Forrest raided Memphis, the Union commander (General Washburn) escaping in his nightshirt, Forrest riding off with the unfortunate man's clothes! Raiding with impunity, Forrest even captured six Union ships on the Tennessee River, until ordered east in November as a reinforcement to General Hood.

26

While Forrest's brilliant little operation was making fools of the Union commanders who opposed him, General Sherman led three Union armies into Georgia, the Armies of the Cumberland, the Tennessee, and the Ohio. Opposing his 99,000 was Johnston's Confederate Army of Tennessee, 60,000 strong, who skilfully retired before Sherman, skirmishing at Dalton (9 May), Resaca (15 May) and Cassville (19 May).

Johnston established himself on Kenesaw Mountain and the surrounding area. Sherman, aiming to capture the important town of Atlanta, tried first a frontal assault (27 June) which was thrown back with heavy losses, then turned the Confederate left, forcing Johnston into a retirement to protect Atlanta. As Johnston's left was again turned, an ungrateful and near-sighted Confederate government relieved Johnston of command. Against far superior forces, Johnston had restricted Sherman's advance to one mile a day while suffering only minor losses himself, a remarkable achievement.

His successor, the impulsive General Hood, attacked the Union forces immediately at Peachtree Creek (20 July); the Confederates were repelled and forced into the defences of Atlanta itself. The impetuous Hood threw out attacks from the defences, at the Battles of Atlanta and Ezra Church (22 and 28 July), losing some 12,300 Confederate troops to only 4,354 Union. Sherman's cavalry, swinging behind Atlanta, failed to cut Confederate rail communications, so Sherman moved his entire force towards the railway lines south of the city. A Confederate counter-attack at Jonesboro (31 August) failed, and Hood was forced to evacuate Atlanta that night.

March to the Sea

As Hood retorted by trying to cut Sherman's own line of communication, Sherman hit upon a unique plan to foil his opponent: he abandoned the line of communication voluntarily rather than use valuable troops to protect it, and marched eastwards with 68,000 men towards Savannah and the coast, living off the country. Cutting a ruthless fifty-mile wide stretch of devastated country to the sea (300 miles away), Sherman destroyed the war-supporting agricultural economy of central Georgia by his 'scorched earth' policy. Arriving before Savannah in December, Sherman stormed Fort McAllister on 13 December, opened communications with Union naval forces off the coast, and forced the Confederate abandonment of the city on 21 December.

Franklin–Nashville Campaign

Hood, meanwhile, tried to divert Sherman's attentions by invading Tennessee with his own and Forrest's army, the latter's detachment being ordered to support Hood. Opposed by General Thomas' Union Army of the Cumberland (detached by Sherman prior to the march through Georgia), Hood advanced, impetuously as ever, until he reached a Union entrenched position at Franklin. Hood threw his army into the attack without any tactical sense, and was repulsed with horrific casualties – 6,300 out of 38,000 engaged (30 November). Franklin was a delaying action which allowed Thomas time to re-organise, re-equip and train new recruits in garrison at Nashville. Hood arrived outside the city on 2 December, but was attacked by Thomas on the 15th. Without Forrest (foolishly sent on a raid), Hood had little chance against Thomas' great superiority; trying to continue the fight next day, Hood's entire army was broken; only 5,300 became casualties, but the remainder became a fleeing rabble. It was the most decisive tactical victory of the war, poor Hood paying the penalty for his imprudent conduct.

The War at Sea, 1864–5

The sinking fortunes of the Confederacy received no relief in the war at sea. The *C.S.S. Hunley*, a submarine 'secret weapon', succeeded in torpedoing and sinking the *U.S.S. Housatonic* in Charleston harbour on 17 February 1864, but sank along with her victim. The Confederate privateer *Alabama*, after an amazing voyage of destruction, was engaged by the *U.S.S. Kearsarge* off Cherbourg on 19 June 1864, and sunk.

On 5 August 1864 Admiral Farragut sailed his U.S. fleet into Mobile Bay in the face of heavy fire, practically ending blockade-running in the Gulf of Mexico. The *C.S.S. Tennessee* bravely tried to take on the entire Union fleet, but was pounded to pieces. On 27 October the powerful Confederate ironclad *Albemarle*, which had wreaked havoc among many Union coastal operations, was attacked by a specially-designed Federal launch; torpedoed, the *Albemarle* sank at Plymouth, North Carolina.

With the *Albemarle* no longer a danger, the Union moved on the last blockade-runners' port, Wilmington, North Carolina. On 23–25 December 1864 Admiral Porter and General Butler led a combined Federal attack on Fort Fisher, the key to Wilmington harbour. After a farcical amphibious landing, Butler withdrew much to Porter's disgust; Grant replaced Butler in command of the army contingent of the expedition with General Terry. Together, Porter and Terry attacked Fort Fisher a second time, on 13–15 January 1865; after a costly assault and bitter Confederate resistance, Fort Fisher surrendered. The last sea-gate of the South was closed. Supplies could no longer come through; the Confederacy was doomed.

The Carolina Campaign

Far too late, President Davis recognised Lee's true abilities and appointed him General-in-Chief, perhaps eighteen months after the time necessary to save the Confederacy. Lee at once restored Johnston to command what remained of Confederate forces in the Carolinas.

Marching from Savannah, Sherman occupied and burnt (probably accidentally) Columbia, South Carolina (17 February 1865). On 22 February a Union amphibious expedition captured Wilmington. Johnston hoped to bolster up the collapsing Confederacy by defeating Sherman's army in detail; at Bentonville (19 March) he surprised and mauled Sherman's left wing, but when the bulk of the vastly superior Union army came up on the following day, Johnston retired having suffered twice as many casualties as he had inflicted. Sherman, having marched 425 miles since leaving Savannah, was joined by the expedition from Wilmington, and rested for three weeks until the muddy roads had become sufficiently dry in spring for him to join Grant outside Petersburg.

Selma Campaign

General Wilson's Federal cavalry corps, 13,500 strong, was detached by Thomas into Alabama to capture the vital Confederate supply-depot at

Selma. Brushing aside Forrest's 3,000 Confederates, Wilson arrived outside the fortifications of Selma in late March. Storming the defences, Forrest and the local militia were overcome (2 April); Wilson destroyed the stores, ammunition dumps and foundries, crossed the Alabama and swept through into Georgia. The noose was tightening rapidly around the Confederacy.

Petersburg, Phase Two

Lee, with 60,000 hungry, ill-equipped men, still held the thirty-seven-mile stretch of entrenchments around the Petersburg–Richmond defence-line. The morale of Lee's outnumbered army was still high, as they demonstrated by repelling yet another Union probe at Hatcher's Run (5–7 February 1865). The situation inside the defence-line was so critical that Lee resolved to abandon the capital and break out with the Army of Northern Virginia, in an attempt to link up with Johnston's force in North Carolina. On 25 March Lee threw almost half his mobile force into an attack on Fort Stedman, in an attempt to break Grant's encirclement and leave a passage open for the Confederate exit. The Fort was taken, but an immediate counter-attack not only recaptured the Union position, but took several Confederate advance-posts as well. Lee lost 4,000, Grant about half as many. The Confederate situation deteriorated even further when Sheridan arrived from the Valley campaign, bringing Grant's strength to 122,000.

On 29 March Grant assaulted the Confederate right; Lee brilliantly counter-attacked and drove the Federals back at Dinwiddie Court House and White Oak Road. On 1 April Sheridan hit the Confederate entrenchments at Five Forks; the southern line collapsed in panic, exposing the entire right of the Confederate army. On 2 April Grant ordered a general advance; as Sherman swept behind Petersburg, three columns smashed through the Confederate lines; General Hill was killed in a vain attempt to rally for a counter-attack. Petersburg itself, aided by reinforcements from Longstreet's corps in Richmond, somehow held on until nightfall. Lee then ordered the evacuation of the Petersburg–Richmond defences.

Appomattox Campaign

Lee tried to join Johnston south of Danville, where President Davis had set up a temporary capital. Harassed all the way, a whole Confederate corps was forced to surrender at the Battle of Sayler's Creek (6–7 April), leaving Lee with barely 30,000 ragged, half-starved troops. Lee's final effort was an attack on the Union advance-guard at Appomattox on 9 April. As the remainder of the Union army came up, Lee realised the hopelessness of the situation and asked for an armistice; Grant accepted the surrender of the Army of Northern Virginia (28,356 strong) at Appomattox Courthouse at 3.45 p.m. on 9 April 1865. To all intents and purposes, the war was over.

Abraham Lincoln had been re-elected to the Presidency of the United States in 1864, due largely to the successes of Grant and Sherman. He realised that the war was reaching its conclusion, and planned the reconstruction of the Union, in the words of his second inaugural address, 'With malice towards none; with charity towards all'. Under Lincoln, the Union could have been reassembled with a minimum of bitterness; but, tragically for the nation, Lincoln was assassinated by John Wilkes Booth, a southern fanatic, as he sat in Ford's Theatre, Washington, on 16 April. The President died next day. Booth and his accomplices were hunted down, Booth dying by bullet, the remainder by hanging.

The last acts of the Confederacy were soon played out; Johnston surrendered to Sherman on 26 April; General Taylor surrendered Confederate forces east of the Mississippi on 4 May. On 10 May President Davis was captured by Wilson's cavalry at Irwinsville, Georgia. The last Confederate contingent under arms was surrendered by General Kirby Smith on 26 May 1865.

On 29 May, Lincoln's successor as President, Andrew Johnson, issued the Proclamation of Amnesty, which officially ended the Civil War, but there remained one Confederate command still at large: the *C.S.S. Shenandoah*, a British-built raider under Commander J. I. Waddell who, unaware of the Confederate surrender, continued to prowl the high seas from the Cape of Good Hope to Australia, and thence north to the Bering Sea, where he effectively destroyed the U.S. whaling industry, sinking twenty-seven ships and capturing five. Learning of the end of the war from a British ship off California, Waddell sailed for England and surrendered his ship at Liverpool on 9 November 1865. The final act of a tragic war was over.

This book is primarily concerned with the most attractive facet of the Civil War: the costumes worn by the participants. But there should never be misconception about the true cost of the Civil War; a brief analysis of figures demonstrates clearly why the echoes of the war can still, perhaps, be heard. Without Lincoln's humanity, the war's bitter taste lingered for generations.

No amount of impersonal figures can convey a hundredth of the cost of the Civil War in terms of human misery and suffering, but those approximations which follow may emphasize the enormity of the tragedy which befell America in the years 1861–65:

	U.S.A.	C.S.A.
Killed in action	67,058	}94,000+?
Died of wounds	43,012	
Died in prison camps	30,156	30,152
Died of disease	224,586	70,000+?
Died of accidents, etc.	24,872	Unrecorded
Wounded in action	300,000+?	235,000+?
Property destruction	$100,000,000	

Highest percentage losses in one action

1st Texas, Antietam	82·3%
1st Minnesota, Gettysburg	82·0%
21st Georgia, Bull Run	76·0%
141st Pennsylvania, Gettysburg	75·7%
101st New York, Bull Run	73·8%
26th North Carolina, Gettysburg	71·7%
25th Massachusetts, Cold Harbor	70·0%
6th Mississippi, Shiloh	70·0%

In a war which incongruously combined almost-Napoleonic tactics with rifled artillery, torpedo, land mine and aerial observation, heavy losses were to be expected; but even at this distance in time the losses which occurred are staggering: Garnett's Virginian brigade entered 'Pickett's charge' at Gettysburg with a strength of 1,427; 486 returned to the Confederate lines. Putting impersonal statistics into more human terms, of the combined uniformed strength of both sides, one man in five was killed and another wounded.

(The descriptive notes on the following colour plates commence on page 135.)

1 Major-General, Full Dress.
(n.b. Painted to represent Maj.-Gen. G. A. Custer.)

2 Brigadier-Generals, Service Dress.

3 a) 1st Lieutenant, Cavalry, Service Dress.
  b) Private, Cavalry, Service Dress.
  c) Corporal, 2nd Cavalry, Full Dress, 1860–61.
(n.b. Figures should be identified from left to right throughout this
section.)

4 a) 1st Sergeant, Cavalry, with Sheridan's Guidon.
  b) Captain, Cavalry, Full Dress.

5 a) Sergeant, Cavalry, with Custer's Guidon.
   b) Officer, 1st Rhode Island Cavalry.

6 a) Private, Cavalry, in 'gum blanket'.
   b) Corporal, Cavalry, with Regimental Standard.

7 a) Corporal, Cavalry, with Company guidon.
   b) Private, Cavalry, with Designating Flag, Army Cavalry Reserve
       Headquarters, Army of the Potomac.

8 Corporal, 6th Pennsylvania Cavalry (Rush's Lancers.)

9 a) Officer, 3rd Pennsylvania Cavalry (60th Volunteers).
   b) Officer, 4th Pennsylvania Cavalry (64th Volunteers).

10 a) Private, 3rd New Jersey Cavalry.
    b) Private, Benton Hussars.

11 a) Officer, 1st Cavalry.
    b) Officer, 9th Vermont Cavalry.
    c) General of Cavalry.

U.S.A.

12 a) Officer, Infantry, Campaign Dress.
   b) Sergeant, 2nd Infantry, Full Dress.
   c) Officer, Infantry, Full Dress.

13 a) Corporal, Infantry, with National Flag.
   b) Musician, Infantry, Full Dress.
   c) Private, Infantry, Full Dress.

U.S.A.

14 a) Private, 22nd New York Militia.
    b) Private, Infantry, in greatcoat.
    c) Officer, Infantry, Service Dress.

15 a) Drum Major, Infantry, Full Dress.
   b) Private, 42nd Pennsylvania Volunteers (Bucktails).
   c) 1st Sergeant, Infantry, Campaign Dress.

16 a) Private, 20th Maine.
   b) Corporal, Iron Brigade, First Uniform.
   c) Private, Iron Brigade, Service Dress.

17 a) Private, 21st Michigan, Service Dress.
    b) Private, Irish Brigade.
    c) Private, 8th Wisconsin, Service Dress.

18 a) Officer, 5th New York Zouaves, Full Dress.
   b) Zouave, Campaign Dress.
   c) Private, 5th New York Zouaves, Full Dress.

19 a) Private, 9th New York Volunteers.
   b) Officer, 9th New York Volunteers.

U.S.A.

20 79th New York Volunteers, 1861.
    a) Private, Full Dress.
    b) Private, Service Dress.
    c) Sergeant, Full Dress.

21 a) Private, 39th New York Volunteers (Garibaldi Guard).
   b) Private, 1st Massachusetts Militia.
   c) Corporal, Vermont Brigade.

22 a) Private, 7th New York National Guard.
   b) Corporal, 7th New York National Guard.
   c) Sergeant, New York Militia.

23 a) Officer, 1st Rhode Island Volunteers.
   b) Private, 1st Rhode Island Volunteers.
   c) Private, 2nd New Hampshire Volunteers.

U.S.A.

24 a) Sergeant, with marker flag, 14th New York Volunteers
    b) Sergeant, Coy 'D', 19th Illinois Volunteers (Ellsworth Zouave
       Cadets).

25 a) Private, 4th Michigan Volunteers.
b) Private, 4th Michigan Volunteers.
c) Officer, 11th Indiana Volunteers.

26 a) Private, 83rd Pennsylvania Volunteers.
   b) Drummer, 114th Pennsylvania Volunteers.
   c) Private, 114th Pennsylvania Volunteers.

27 U.S.A.: 1st Sharpshooters.
 a) Officer
 b) Corporal

28 a) Sergeant, 1st Heavy Artillery, Corps d'Afrique.
   b) 1st Sergeant, 56th U.S. Coloured Infantry.
   c) Private, U.S. Coloured Infantry.

29 a) Drummer, 1st Artillery.
    b) Private, 1st Artillery.

30 a) 1st Lieutenant, 2nd Artillery, Service Dress, 1862.
   b) 1st Lieutenant, 14th Ohio Volunteer Light Artillery, 1864.
   c) Gunner, Light Artillery, Full Dress.

31 a) U.S. Ordnance Sergeant, Full Dress.
    b) 1st Sergeant, U.S. Engineers, Full Dress.

U.S.A.

32 a) Hospital Steward, Full Dress.
   b) Lieutenant-Colonel Surgeon, in overcoat.

33 a) Private 4th New Hampshire Regiment.
   b) Private, 22nd New York Regiment.
   c) Captain, Invalid Corps.

34 a) General, Full Dress.
   b) Major, Engineers, Full Dress.
   c) Brigadier-General.

35 a) Major, Cavalry.
   b) General of Cavalry.

36 Private, Cavalry, Campaign Dress.

37 a) Corporal, Cavalry, Full Dress, with Guidon.
   b) Sergeant, 1st Virginia Cavalry.

38 a) Sergeant, 1st Texas Cavalry, 1861.
    b) Private, Charleston Light Dragoons, 1860.

39 a) Private, 26th Texas Cavalry (Debray's Mounted Rifleman).
    b) Private, Texas Cavalry, with Guidon.
    c) Private, 1st Kentucky Cavalry Brigade.

40 a) Private, Georgia Governor's Horse Guard, 1861.
    b) Private, Southern Militia, 1860–61.

41 a) Private, Sussex Light Dragoons, 1861.
   b) Captain, Sussex Light Dragoons, 1861.

C.S.A.

42 a) 1st Lieutenant, Hampton's Legion.
    b) 1st Sergeant, Beaufort Troop.

43 8th Texas Cavalry
   a) Private, Campaign Dress.
   b) Private, Regulation Dress.

44 a) Major, Infantry, Full Dress.
   b) Colonel, 20th Alabama Regiment.
   c) 2nd Lieutenant, Infantry, Campaign Dress.

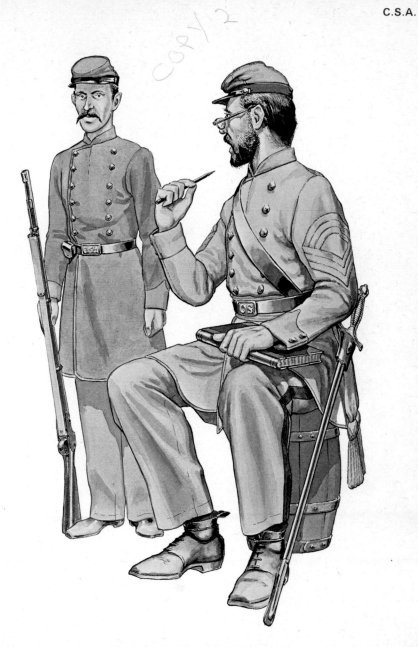

45 a) Private, Infantry, Full Dress.
   b) Sergeant-Major, Infantry, Full Dress.

46 Privates, Infantry, Service Dress.

47 a) Private, Infantry.
   b) Private, Infantry.
   c) Private, Company 'B', 15th Virginia Infantry.

48 a) Corporal, Infantry, with 1st National Flag.
   b) Private, Infantry, with Battle Flag.

49 a) Sergeant, Texas Infantry, with State Flag, 1863.
   b) Sergeant-Major, South Carolina Volunteers, with State Flag
      1861.

50 a) Private, Sumter Light Guard.
   b) Bass Drummer, Sumter Light Guard.
   c) Officer, Sumter Light Guard.

51 a) Private, Company 'E', 23rd Virginia Volunteers, Service Dress.
   b) Private, ditto, Full Dress.
   c) Private, Savannah Volunteer Guard, Full Dress.

52 a) Private, Maryland Guard Zouaves.
b) Private, Company 'A', 5th Georgia Regiment, Service Dress.
c) Private, ditto, Full Dress.

53 a) Private, Alexandria Rifles.
   b) Private, Woodis Rifles, Full Dress.
   c) Drum Major, 1st Virginia Volunteers, Full Dress.

54 Privates, Louisiana Tiger Zouaves.

55 1st Battalion Louisiana Zouaves.
   a) Private.
   b) 1st Lieutenant.

56 a) Private, McClellan's Zouaves.
   b) Private, Chichester Zouave Cadets.
   c) Cadet, Virginia Military Institute.

57 4th Texas Volunteers.
   a) Sergeant, Company 'B'.
   b) Private, Company 'H'.
   c) Private, Company 'A'.

C.S.A.

58 3rd Texas Infantry.
   a) Private, Campaign Dress.
   b) Corporal, Campaign Dress.

59 Infantry in 'Butternut', 1865.

60 Artillery.
  a) Captain, Full Dress.
  b) Gunner, Service Dress.

61 a) 2nd Lieutenant, Washington Artillery
   b) Officer, 'A' Battery, 1st Tennessee Light Artillery (Rutledge's
        Battery).

C.S.A.

62 a) Private, Rifle Volunteers.
    b) Private, Palmetto Guards.
    c) Private, Infantry Volunteers.

63 a) Commander, U.S. Navy, Summer Campaign Dress, 1862.
   b) Captain, U.S. Navy, Undress, 1862.

64 a) Seaman, Confederate Navy.
    b) Petty Officer, U.S. Navy, Summer Dress.

THE ARMIES OF THE CIVIL WAR

In the early part of the Civil War, both sides relied largely upon the volunteer and militia companies which were already in existence prior to the outbreak of war. These companies, many half-trained and hardly a man ever having seen a shot fired in anger (except the veterans of the Mexican War), were 'regimented' into battalions for active service, often each company wearing a different uniform to the rest of the battalion. As an example, the 6th Regiment of Massachusetts Volunteer Militia of 1860 may be cited: each company as was customary wore its own uniform and bore its own title.

'A' Company – Lawrence Cadets. Blue frock-coats and pantaloons, white crossbelts.
'B' Company – Groton Artillery. Dark blue frock-coats and light blue trousers.
'C' Company – Mechanic Phalanx. Grey with yellow trimming.
'D' Company – City Guards. Grey with buff trimming.
'E' Company – Davis Guards. Dark blue frock-coats and light blue trousers.
'F' Company – Warren Light Guard. Dark blue frock-coats and light blue trousers.
'G' Company – Worcester Light Infantry. 'Full dress uniforms of blue'.
'H' Company – Watson Light Guards. Grey.
'I' Company – Lawrence Light Infantry. Blue frock-coats, red trousers, French-style képi.
'K' Company – Washington Artillery. Grey.

Many companies of larger formations on both sides bore individual names of the most outlandish character: included among the most bizarre were the Mississippi Yankee Hunters, Mounted Wild Cats, New Garden Fearnoughts, Nickelsville Spartan Band, Pee Dee Wild Cats, Tyranny Unmasked Artillery, Hook and Ladder Guard, Clinch Mountain Boomers, Scuppernong Greys, Cherokee Stone Walls, Franklin Fire Eaters, Knights of the Border, Hell Roaring Horse and the One-Eyed Battalion!

A typical Union infantry regiment at full strength consisted of ten companies, each of ninety-seven men and three officers: one captain, one 1st lieutenant, one 2nd lieutenant, one 1st sergeant, four sergeants, eight corporals, two musicians, one waggoner and eighty-two privates. Regimental staff consisted of one colonel, one lieutenant-colonel, one major, one adjutant (a lieutenant), one quartermaster (lieutenant), one surgeon, one assistant-surgeon, one sergeant-major, one regimental quartermaster-sergeant, one regimental commissary-sergeant, one hospital steward, two musicians, and twenty-four bandsmen (band later abolished). Average strengths, however, varied from about 500 down to 150. Confederate regiments were similar in composition.

When Union regiments reached the level of 150–200 effectives, they were usually broken up into new formations; Confederate regiments, however, were never drafted but retained the original cadre and built up from recruits. This established a vital *esprit de corps* which kept morale higher than that of the typical Union regiment, a policy which was continued by the brigading together of regiments from one state.

Roughly, Union cavalry regiments (after 1862) consisted of twelve troops. Each troop comprised one captain, one 1st lieutenant, one 2nd lieutenant (plus one supernumery lieutenant prior to 1863), with between 82 and 100 men including one 1st sergeant, one quarter-master-sergeant, one commissary-sergeant, five sergeants, eight corporals, two teamsters, two farriers, one saddler, one waggoner, and two musicians. Regimental staff consisted of one colonel, one lieu-tenant-colonel, three majors, one adjutant (lieutenant), one commissary (lieutenant), one quartermaster (lieutenant), one surgeon, one assistant-surgeon, one sergeant-major, one quartermaster-sergeant, one commissary-sergeant, one saddler-sergeant, one chief farrier (black-smith), and two hospital stewards. As in the infantry, actual strength was generally well below establishment; Confederate regiments were similarly organised.

The Confederacy revived the old European-style 'legions' for a brief period, this term being applied to regimental combinations of infantry, cavalry and often artillery; in effect, a tiny miniature army of regi-mental strength, capable of operating independently of any support.

Artillery organisation varied considerably, batteries varying between six and four guns each, the weight and type of gun usually varying within the individual battery. Each gun was usually manned by six or seven men, and was complete with limber and caisson (ammunition-waggon), each drawn by a six-horse team. Each battery was equipped with travelling forge, extra caissons and baggage-waggons. In addition to the battery staff (comprising musicians and skilled artificers) there was, whenever possible, an excess of men to man the guns, in order that the battery would have sufficient crew to keep firing in action even after sustaining considerable casualties.

Brigades were formed of two or more regiments, the average brigade strength being four to five regiments. Two or more brigades formed a division; at Chancellorsville for example, Federal divisions averaged 6,200 men and Confederate 8,700. Two or more divisions formed a corps. Standard organisation on the Union side consisted of forty-five infantry regiments and nine batteries of light artillery (nine brigades organised in three divisions). Two or more corps comprised an army, those of the Union taking their name from the river which flowed in the Department in which the army was organised, while the Confederates generally named their armies from the state. This rule, however, was loosely applied as can be seen from the following list of the sixteen Federal and twenty-three Confederate armies which existed as independent 'operational organisations':

Federal: Army of the Cumberland, the Frontier, Georgia, the Gulf, the James, Kansas, the Mississippi, the Mountain Department, the Ohio, the Potomac, the Shenandoah, the South-west, Virginia, West Tennessee, West Virginia.

Confederate: Central Kentucky, East Tennessee, Eastern Kentucky, the Kanawha, Kentucky, Louisiana, Middle Tennessee, the Mississippi, Missouri, Mobile, New Mexico, Northern Virginia, the North-west, the Peninsula, Pensacola, the Potomac, the Shenandoah, the South-west, Tennessee, Trans-Mississippi Department, Vicksburg, the West, West Tennessee.

In the Union army a total of 2,128,948 men are known to have served, of whom 75,215 were regulars, 1,933,779 were volunteers, 46,347 were drafted, and 73,607 were draft-substitutes. Confederate records are less precise; between 1,227,890 and 1,406,180 men enlisted during the war. These figures represent approximately one in eleven and one in nine respectively of the total population of all ages, races and both sexes.

One point often forgotten is the extreme youth of many of the combatants, a fact which is partly disguised by the fashion of growing heavy beards prevalent in both armies, thereby providing deceiving photographs. Of the Union troops, it is known that at least 100,000 were sixteen years of age, and another 100,000 were fifteen; in other words, almost one in ten Federals was sixteen or less. No similar figures are available for the Confederacy, but it is likely that an even larger percentage (particularly in the later stages of the war) were of a similar age-group. At New Market (1864) the cadets of the Virginia Military Institute formed part of the Confederate battle-line.

John Clem, a private in the 22nd Michigan, was twelve years old 'and small even for his age' when at Chickamauga he was attacked by a Confederate colonel. Clem shot the officer dead. To protect the boy from further danger, (his hat was pierced by three bullets that day), Rosecrans promoted him to sergeant and assigned him to 'special duty' at headquarters. How many more Clems suffered the fate of their elders at the hands of bullet and shrapnel?

UNIFORMS OF THE CIVIL WAR

At the outbreak of war, the Union army had an existing set of Dress Regulations, but the Confederacy had to write their own. As the Confederate army was based initially upon the local volunteers and militia, whose uniforms of 'cadet grey' were popular for such corps throughout the country, the South wisely decided (in the first Dress Regulations of September 1861) to authorise this colour as the standard for their army. Those Union regiments which were also dressed in grey were re-uniformed as soon as possible in order to prevent confusion occurring amid the smoke of battle.

The volunteer companies of both sides often dressed themselves in elaborate and quite impractical costumes, which soon became modified (officially or otherwise) when serious campaigning began. The soldiers of both armies had the good sense (or sometimes improvidence) to make their cumbersome equipment as comfortable and easy to carry as possible, often to the extent of throwing away valuable items – as the chills of winter came on, many a soldier regretted discarding his great-coat to save weight in the summer!

Gradually, the armies became progressively more unkempt and dishevelled as all attempts at martial bearing gave way to comfort and utility. The knapsack, for example, disappeared rapidly in some regiments: 'It was inconvenient to change the underwear too often . . . the better way was to dress out and out, and wear that outfit until the enemy's knapsacks, or the folks at home supplied a change.' Eventually, 'Reduced to the minimum, the private soldier consisted of one man, one hat, one jacket, one shirt, one pair of pants, one pair of drawers, one pair of shoes and one pair of socks. His baggage was one blanket, one rubber blanket, and one haversack'.

Even the water canteen (or, in Confederate cases, often a wooden barrel) were 'as a general thing discarded . . . A good strong tin cup was found better . . . easier to fill at a well or spring, and was serviceable as a boiler for making coffee'. The metal canteens were frequently split in half to make two frying-pans!

Of the regulation equipment, only the haversack was universally retained: the 'odorous haversack, which often stinks with its mixture of bacon, salt junk, sugar, coffee, tea, desicated vegetables, rice, bits of yesterday's dinner, and old scraps . . .' Other equipment was carried rolled in the blanket over one shoulder.

Numerous units of both sides were dressed in ornate uniforms styled after the French zouaves and chasseurs à pied, European élite troops which both armies liked to emulate. Their impractical dress was soon modified, but surprisingly the *esprit de corps* of many such units resulted in their keeping the distinctive costume wherever possible, no matter how incongruous baggy Cossack-style trousers and Arabian turbans might appear!

As uniforms gradually became functional instead of decorative, many soldiers – in particular officers – designed their own costumes so that they assumed an almost civilian appearance, long overcoats, coloured waistcoats and straw hats being popular. Some officers, like Ulysses S. Grant, achieved an almost disreputable appearance; Grant often wore a shabby private's jacket with General's rank bars sewn on, and a battered felt hat. An English witness to the Battle of Chattanooga, Henry Yates Thompson, wrote in amazement of how Grant was dressed in 'plain citizen's clothes . . . wearing nothing military about him except a large opera glass'. Grant wore 'a black surtout with black braid on and quite loose, black trousers and a black wideawake hat and thin Wellington boots'. General Hunter, standing next to Grant, was similarly dressed, except that 'his black wideawake having gold cord around it but having the brim turned down all round over his cadaverous face'.

Other Generals, like George A. Custer, designed their own, ornate uniforms with ludicrous amounts of gold braid: described as 'a circus rider gone mad', Custer's favourite suit was made entirely of black velvet, with a blue sailor-collar, the whole half-covered in gold embroidery. The black felt campaign-hat soon lost its shape, so that many Union troops took on a ridiculous appearance – a limp, sagging affair down around the ears, blocked-up like a shabby top hat, squashed down like a straw 'boater' or punched up; General Burnside wore his hat with the crown in this latter fashion, so that it resembled a tall dunce's cap! The practice of wearing civilian clothes was naturally confusing and sometimes fatal; at Logan Cross Roads, Confederate General Felix Zollicoffer apparently mistook a body of Federal troops for his own, and rode up to speak to their commanding officer. Zollicoffer was wearing a white raincoat so voluminous that it completely covered his uniform, and it was only after several minutes conversation that the Union officer realised who Zollicoffer was – and shot him dead!

In addition to the personal idiosyncracies of many officers and men, an additional factor – which brought about the most radical change in the appearance of the uniforms of the war – was the Union blockade which caused desperate shortages among the Confederate army. Such was the situation that it is doubtful whether the correct regulation uniform was *ever* worn in large numbers (if at all), but by the middle of the war the troops of the Confederacy were dressed in a mixture of what few regulation uniforms were available, much captured Federal costume, purely civilian dress, and home-dyed uniforms, which, the supply of grey dye having run out, were of a light brown, buff or yellowish tone known as 'butternut', the dye being made from boiled nutshells and iron oxide (rust). With this costume was worn large quantities of civilian clothes until soldiers lost all resemblance to members of a military unit; shoes were improvised by nailing leather onto wooden soles, using horse-shoes as boot-irons, or as one Confederate wrote: 'Shoes are very scarce. The men get pieces of raw hide from the butchers, and, after wrapping their feet up in old rags, sew the hide around them . . . which they wear until it wears out'.

Corpse-robbing, a repellent but extremely common habit, led to a large proportion of the Confederate army wearing Federal light blue trousers and captured boots; so popular did this practice become that soon Confederate regiments were wearing Union head-dress and jackets as well! Officers tried to prevent such large-scale appropriation of Union uniforms as it could cause tactical problems (both sides assuming the same basic appearance) as well as difficulties concerning captured Confederates who could officially have been regarded as spies. Official disapproval (except in cases of absolute necessity) of robbing the dead often restricted Confederate 'appropriations' to trousers, boots and miscellaneous equipment.

The expected wear-and-tear of campaigning was not the only reason why uniforms quickly became ragged or wore out entirely; many uniforms (particularly at the beginning of the war) were made of a material called 'shoddy', which was described by the magazine *Harper's Weekly* (perhaps the most popular reading-matter of the two armies during the war)as 'a villainous compound, the refuse stuff and sweepings of the shop, pounded, rolled, glued, and smoothed to the external form and gloss of cloth, but no more like the genuine article than the shadow is to the substance . . . soldiers, on the first day's march or in the earliest storm, found their clothes, overcoats and blankets, scattering to the wind in rags, or dissolving into their primitive elements of dust under the pelting rain.'

In actual fact, the term 'full dress' was not used at the time, but is used here for the sake of convenience, to signify the ornate regulation uniform, as being different from the fatigue dress worn almost invariably (after the first few months of the war) on campaign.

RANK MARKINGS

Rank markings, whilst varying between the two armies, were of the same basic style, though the following details should not be regarded as universal: it was not uncommon to find Union officers wearing Confederate-style rank-markings and vice-versa. Such distinctions as the arrangement of buttons, sashes, etc. which were also indicative of rank will be found in the text to the individual plates which illustrate these details.

Non-commissioned Officers (both armies)

Corporal – two chevrons, worn on upper sleeve.
Sergeant – three chevrons.
1st Sergeant – three chevrons with a lace lozenge above.
Ordnance-Sergeant – three chevrons with a five-pointed star above.
Quartermaster-Sergeant – three chevrons with a horizontal 'tie' of lace linking the upper corners.
Sergeant-Major – three chevrons, with an arc of lace linking the upper corners.

Officers (Union)

Rank indicated by laced shoulder-bars on a backing of cloth of the colour of the arm of service (cavalry yellow, infantry light blue, artillery red) with rank-bars thereon; in full dress, similar badges on gold lace epaulettes except where otherwise stated below:
2nd Lieutenant – No rank-badges on epaulettes or shoulder-bars.
1st Lieutenant – One gold bar at either end of shoulder-bar; one silver bar on epaulette.
Captain – Two gold bars on shoulder-bars; two silver bars on epaulette.
Major – Gold oak-leaf on shoulder-bars, epaulettes plain.
Lieutenant-Colonel – Silver oak-leaf at either end of shoulder-bars and on epaulettes.

Colonel – Silver eagle.
Brigadier-General – One silver star.
Major-General – Two silver stars.
Lieutenant-General – Three silver stars.

Officers (Confederate)

Rank indicated in three ways – by thickness of lace decoration on sleeve-cuff and képi, and by gold rank-badges on either side of collar.
2nd Lieutenant – One bar on collar, one braid on képi.
1st Lieutenant – Two bars on collar, one braid.
Captain – Three bars on collar, two braids.
Major – One star on collar, three braids.
Lieutenant-Colonel – Two stars on collar, three braids.
Colonel – Three stars on collar, three braids.
General (all ranks) – Three stars in laurel-wreath on collar, four braids.

BELT-PLATES AND BUTTONS

No universal rules can be established for the designs of waist- and shoulder-belt plates worn by both armies; plain brass buckles were popular in the Confederacy and as the Union blockade tightened shortages became desperate.

The regulation belt-plate for both officers and men of the Federal army consisted of the heraldic crest of the United States, an eagle with outspread wings surrounded by wreaths and star-constellation. The pattern usually worn by Union enlisted men was oval, bearing the letters 'u.s.'; on the shoulder-belt the plate was circular, bearing the American eagle. Almost without exception, all belt-plates were made of brass (gilt and silver for officers). The more common regulation Confederate pattern was (for officers) a circular belt-clasp of the letters 'c.s.' often surrounded by stars, inside one or two wreaths; for other ranks, a rectangular plate bearing the letters 'c.s.a.', or rectangular with rounded corners bearing 'c.s.'.

Many Confederate belt-plates were manufactured in Europe, and numerous semi-official patterns are still in existence: circular clasps with lion-head motif, rectangular plates bearing the Battle Flag surrounded by a laurel wreath – even copies of Union designs. The Confederacy also used many pre-war militia plates, and, of course, a large quantity of captured Union items – often worn with the 'U.S.' lettering upside-down.

Both armies used 'state' belt-plates, as worn by the militia and volunteers before the war. Some New York units, for example, wore oval plates bearing the letters 'S.N.Y.' (State of New York), while other (rectangular) examples included the words 'VIRGINIA' or 'VA' (Virginia), 'S.C.' (South Carolina) and 'N.C.' (North Carolina), the letters often being surrounded by wreaths. Plates also bore state emblems – the Palmetto tree and the Texas 'Lone Star' were popular.

Numerous 'regimental' plates also existed – the New York National Guard for example wore plates bearing the letters 'N.G.', whilst some Confederate units of Scottish background even had plates decorated with a border of thistles, with the unit title stamped in the middle, for example 'Scotch Greys Artillery', 'Scotch Rifle Guards', etc. Unfortunately, any study of belt-plates of the Civil War is complicated by the large numbers of fakes and 're-strikes' which were produced decades after the end of the war.

Many of the above notes also apply to the design of buttons used by both armies. Union enlisted men's brass buttons bore the American eagle with wings outstretched, but the gilt buttons of the officers had 'arm of service' distinctions, usually having the letters 'C', 'I', or 'A' for Cavalry, Infantry, and Artillery, placed upon the shield on the eagle's breast. The Engineer corps had a design of an eagle flying over a fortress, the Ordnance one of crossed cannons and the corps title, while those of the Topographical Engineers bore a shield over the letters 'T.E.' in Gothic letters. Musicians' buttons were distinguished by the design of a large lyre; in addition, there existed numerous regimental patterns, many based upon the state seal; the Rhode Island Militia, for example, had buttons bearing the anchor device.

Confederate General officers' buttons bore an eagle with outstretched wings, though without the trappings of the Union version. Engineer officers' buttons bore the letter 'E' in Gothic lettering, whilst those of Cavalry, Infantry, Artillery and Riflemen bore the plain block letters 'C', 'I', 'A' and 'R' respectively. Enlisted men of the artillery had buttons of a similar design to those of the officers; those of all other branches bore the number of the regiment upon their buttons. Each state, however, and including the 'border states' of Maryland and Missouri which supplied regiments to both sides, had their own design of button, almost invariably based upon that state seal, though those of Florida appear to have been of an eagle design not representative of the state crest. Notable among such designs was the ever-present 'Lone Star' of Texas, a similar design for Mississippi with the state name around the edge, the pelican of Louisiana, the Palmetto tree of South Carolina, a sunburst with the letters 'N.C.' in the middle for North Carolina, and the proud 'Sic Semper Tyrannis' motto of Virginia. As shortages became more desperate, the Confederate army took to wearing captured Union buttons, sometimes covered with cloth to hide the design, but many were forced into providing 'home-made' buttons carved from bone, wood and even acorns!

FEDERAL CORPS BADGES

The use of distinctive badges to identify individual military formations within armies dates back to the heraldry of the medieval period and to the 'field signs' used in seventeenth-century warfare. Such distinctive features were later restricted to the members of individual regiments, existing today as the regimental badges worn by many armies. The use of badges to identify larger formations, however (corps and division, etc.), which reached its zenith in the heraldry of the Second World War, originated with the adoption by the U.S. Army of cloth hat-badges in 1863, each Union corps having a distinctive pattern.

The Washington Artillery apparently wore red flannel strips as unit identification at First Bull Run, but this can hardly be classed as a 'formation' badge, though an unusual distinction at the time; the first true 'corps' badges originated when Philip Kearney ordered his men (3rd Division, III Corps) in 1862 to wear a piece of red cloth on the front of their caps to identify them from other members of the Union army. When Hooker assumed command of the Army of the Potomac, he ordered that all his corps be thus identified, and credit for the designing of many of the various insignia goes to General Daniel Butterfield. The badges were stamped from flannel, about $1\frac{1}{2}$ inches across (the size varied), and were fastened to the képis of the various corps, usually on the crown which, from the practice of allowing the cap to 'slouch' down, was visible from the front; and on the front of the felt hat. Thin stamped metal versions of the distinctive badges were not unknown, and officers' badges were sometimes produced in metallic thread.

The badges appeared in the Army of the Potomac in spring 1863, but not in the West until the following year. A story is told of how a veteran of the XV Corps first saw men of the XII Corps, each wearing a star on his cap, whereupon he joked: 'You boys all generals?' When asked about his own corps insignia (the XV Corps not having received theirs), he slapped his cartridge-box and said it was 'Forty rounds in the cartridge box and twenty in the pocket'. General Logan heard about the story, and so was born the design of XV Corps' distinctive badge. Another story refers to the XIV Corps' nickname of 'the acorn boys', which originated when the men were so short of rations that they ate roasted acorns; when the time came to choose a corps distinctive badge, it was an acorn which was selected to commemorate the event.

Some time after Corps badges were prescribed, it became usual to indicate individual divisions within the corps by varying the colouring of the design, the 1st, 2nd and 3rd Divisions having badges of red, white and blue respectively. If a 4th or 5th Division existed, another colour (usually green or orange) was used.

A list of designs of Corps badges follows:

I	Circular disc or an open ring.
II	Trefoil (club).
III	Lozenge (diamond).
IV	Triangle with two equal sides and a longer base.
V	Cross Pattée.
VI	Saltaire (diagonal) cross.
VII	Inverted crescent (points down) with a five-pointed star between the points.
VIII	Six-pointed star.
IX	Shield bearing a crossed anchor and cannon-barrel.
X	Plan of a square bastion; or alternatively, a square with the figure '10' thereon.
XI	Crescent.
XII	Five-pointed star.
XIII	No badge worn.
XIV	Acorn.
XV	Black cartridge-box with or without the lettering 'FORTY ROUNDS'; on a square of the Divisional colour.
XVI	Crossed cannon-barrels; or a saltaire cross pattée, with rounded corners.
XVII	Arrow.
XVIII	Trefoil cross; or a square with the figure '18' thereon.
XIX	Cross pattée with the centre arms joined by a circle; with or without the numeral '19' in the centre.

XX Five-pointed star.
XXI No badge worn.
XXII Pentagon (five-armed) cross.
XXIII Shield, separated by an inverted 'y' into three sections.
XXIV Heart, with or without the figures '24' in the centre.
XXV Lozenge within a square.

ARTILLERY OF THE CIVIL WAR

FIELDPIECES

(All ranges given are approximate, and are those attained with a barrel-elevation of 5 degrees. Calibre specifications refer to inches.)

12-pounder 'Napoleon' gun-howitzer, model 1857. Smoothbore, cal. 4.62. Rate of fire: two aimed shots or four canister per minute. Maximum range 2,000 yards. 'Workhorse' of the Civil War; used extensively by both sides. Reliable and most effective. Also existed in 6-pounder version.

6-pounder, model 1841–44. Smoothbore, cal. 3.67. Range 1,523 yards. Used almost exclusively by the Confederacy; ineffective, replaced wherever possible by 12-pounder smoothbores and 3-inch rifles. Lee recommended that all 6-pounders should be melted down to make 12-pounders.

12-pounder, model 1841–44. Smoothbore, cal. 4.62. Range 1,663 yards. Used by both sides; performance similar to the Napoleon but weighed 530 pounds heavier, therefore not as convenient.

12-pounder Howitzer, model 1841–44. Smoothbore, cal. 4.62. Weight of shot 8.9 pounds. Range 1,072 yards.

24-pounder, model 1841–44. Smoothbore, cal. 5.82. Weight of shot 18.4 pounds. Range 1,322 yards.

32-pounder Howitzer, model 1841–44. Smoothbore, cal. 6.2. Weight of shot 25.60 pounds. Range 1,504 yards.

12-pounder Mountain Howitzer. Lightweight, carried on mule-back. Could be assembled and one round fired in one minute. Range 900 yards.

10-pounder Parrott. Rifled, cal. 3.00. Range 1,900 yards. Used by both sides; found to be ineffective, replaced wherever possible by 3-inch Rodman.

20-pounder Parrott. Rifled, cal. 3.67. Range 1,900 yards (maximum range 3,500 yards). Basic rifled fieldpiece in common usage by both sides.

3-inch Rodman (Ordnance Gun). Rifled, cal. 3.00. Developed by U.S. Ordnance Dept 1863; 10-pounder Parrotts were modified to take same ammunition. Range 1,830 yards; maximum range 4,000 yards. Popular: favoured by Horse Artillery.

12-pounder James. Rifled, cal. 3.67. Range 1,700 yards. Not in common usage.

24-pounder James. Rifled, cal. 4.62. Range 1,800 yards. Not in common usage.

6-pounder Wiard. Rifled, cal. 2.56. Range 1,800 yards.

10-pounder Wiard. Rifled, cal. 3.00. Range 1,850 yards.

6-pounder Whitworth. Rifled, cal. 2.15. Range 2,750 yards. English-made, used by the Confederacy. Used largely solid shot, as long, thin shape of shell (known as a 'bolt') did not permit a sufficient quantity of powder to be inserted to make an effective explosive shell.

12-pounder Whitworth. Rifled, cal. 2.75. Breech-loading, range 2,800 yards (maximum range almost 6 miles). Muzzle-loading version, range 3,000 yards. English-made, used by the Confederacy; exceptional accuracy and performance.

12-pounder Blakely. Rifled, cal. 3.40. Range 1,850 yards. English-made, used in small numbers by the Confederacy; Wade Hampton bought a battery at his own expense. Also larger version: one battery used by South Carolina for coastal defence. Several types of shell used, including flanged and studded projectiles. Exceptional accuracy, though unpopular because of large recoil. Blakely breech-loaders saw little service.

12-pounder Armstrong. Breech-loading, rifled, cal. 3.00. Range 2,100 yards. English-made, exceptional accuracy. Muzzle-loading version had range of 2,200 yards. Breech-loader shell had lead driving bands around case, muzzle-loader had three rows of brass studs. 16-pounder and 4-inch versions produced in small numbers. A number of Armstrongs used by Confederacy.

Confederate Mt. Rifle. Cal. 2.25. Weight of projectile 3 pounds. Range 1,100 yards.

Brooke Gun. Invented by J. M. Brooke, Chief of Confederate Naval Ordnance. Rifled, resembling Parrott with Blakely rifling. Various calibres, including 3-inch fieldpieces firing 10-pound shells. Maximum range 3,500 yards.

SIEGE AND GARRISON ARTILLERY

Not always used for siege work; for example, siege trains used in action at Shiloh and Malvern Hill. Only more important patterns listed below:

Gun	Cal.	Weight of projectile (lbs)	Range (yards)
4½-inch muzzle-loader, rifled	4.5	33	2,078
30-pounder Parrott rifled muzzle-loader	4.2	29	2,200
24-pounder smoothbore	5.82	24	1,900
18-pounder smoothbore	5.3	18.5	1,592
12-pounder smoothbore	4.62	12.3	1,834
8-inch smoothbore Howitzer	8	50.5	1,241

SEACOAST ARTILLERY

Immense in size, used for firing from fixed positions. Largest (20-inch Rodman) weighted 117,000 pounds.

Gun	Cal.	Weight of projectile (lbs)	Range (yards)
32-pounder smoothbore	6.4	32.6	1,922
42-pounder smoothbore	7	42.7	1,955
8-inch Columbiad smoothbore	8	65	1,813
10-inch Columbiad smoothbore	10	128	1,814
15-inch Columbiad smoothbore	15	350	5,730
20-inch Rodman smoothbore	20	1,080	3½ miles
100-pounder Parrott rifled muzzle-loader	6.4	70–100	2,370
200-pounder Parrott rifled muzzle-loader	8	132–175	2,000
300-pounder Parrott rifled muzzle-loader	10	230–250	2,500
80-pounder Whitworth rifled muzzle-loader	5	80	13,665
70-pounder Armstrong rifled breech-loader	6.4	79.8	2,183
8-inch Blakely rifled muzzle-loader	8	200	
150-pounder Armstrong rifled muzzle-loader	8.5	150	
12¾-inch Blakely rifled muzzle-loader	12.75	700	

NAVAL ARTILLERY

Naval guns are outside the scope of this book, but many naval 12-pounder Howitzers were mounted on field carriages for use in amphibious landing operations; cal. 4.6, projectile weight 10 pounds, range 1,085 yards.

MORTARS

Cumbersome to transport, mortars were used only for siege work and garrison duty, on occasion being mounted on railway flatcars for the former purpose, the most famous being the 'Dictator' used by the Federals at Petersburg.

Mortar	Weight of projectile (lbs)	Range (45-degree elevation) (yards)
8-inch mortar	44.5	1,200
10-inch mortar	87.5	2,100
24-pounder Coehorn (bore 5.82 inches)	17	1,200
10-inch garrison mortar	87.5	4,250
13-inch mortar	220	4,325

ROCKETS

A limited number of Congreve rockets were used by the Confederacy; they were no more reliable or accurate than the earlier version employed by the British army at Leipzig and Waterloo: of little use; some used by J. E. B. Stuart. The Federals had Hale rockets, of two sizes, 6- and 16-pounders, maximum range 2,200 yards, with explosive or incendiary heads. More reliable than the Congreve, but still unpopular and generally unserviceable.

GRENADES

Large numbers of explosive grenades were used in the war; over 90,000 Ketcham grenades were purchased by the U.S. Government. Other types: Adams and Excelsior, the latter most unpopular because of the risk of exploding before being thrown. In addition, thousands of rounds of 6-pound spherical shell were used as grenades by being rolled down inclines after the fuse was ignited.

A few experimental cannon were designed by both sides; Union troops captured a Winans steam-gun in 1861, an unlikely contraption using steam as a propellant. Tappey & Lumsden of Petersburg, Virginia, cast a pair of revolving cannon (like a huge revolver on wheels); one blew up and killed the crew during tests. The Confederacy also had a double-barrelled cannon, consisting of two 6-pounder barrels joined together, intended to fire two roundshot connected by a chain which, it was thought, would mow down the enemy. All it achieved in tests was to demolish the chimney of a log cabin, cut down some saplings, and kill a cow!

COMPARISON OF ARTILLERY

Although the best rifled cannon were up to fifty times as accurate as the ordinary smoothbore, some artillerymen preferred the latter; when firing explosive shot, the rifled guns drove their projectiles so deep into the ground that when the shell burst, no splinters penetrated through the surface of the ground: General Imboden recalled that at Bull Run, the ground he occupied 'looked as though a drove of hogs had been rooting there for potatoes' from the shells exploding below ground, causing no casualties. The smoothbores compensated for their defects in accuracy by never burying their shells. Imboden claimed that one battery of smoothbores was worth two of rifled cannon. This is perhaps a rather extreme view, but certainly at close range, firing canister and grapeshot, the Napoleon and other smoothbored guns had no equal.

MACHINE-GUNS

Several designs of machine- and volley-guns were used with mixed effect by both sides.

Williams Gun. The first machine-gun to be used in action, the Confederate 'secret weapon' was invented by Captain R. S. Williams. Single barrel, breech-loader, 1-inch bore, it fired paper cartridges and was mounted on a small mountain howitzer carriage. Range 2,000 yards. First used at Seven Pines (31 May 1862), several batteries of six guns each were ordered by the Confederacy; apparently seven such batteries were completed. Firing 18 to 20 shots per minute, the breech was prone to expansion when hot, causing jamming. Despite this, results were impressive and the gun was considered quite reliable.

Agar Gun. The 'Union Repeating Gun', otherwise known as 'Coffee Mill'. Single barrel, fired .58 cal. bullet, 120 rounds per minute. Mounted on light wheeled carriage, with shield to protect gunners from small-arms fire. Adopted only on Lincoln's personal insistance, these guns were unpopular, though apparently effective; two guns of the 28th Pennsylvania Volunteers at Middleburg, Virginia (29 March 1862) shot up two squadrons of Confederate cavalry at 800 yards, but were then returned to Washington as 'unreliable and unsafe to operate'. Though Confederate witnesses testified to their effectiveness, the Agar Gun was relegated to static defence works.

Gatling Gun. The 1862 model (6-barrel, .58 cal., 250 rounds per minute) was vastly inferior to the much-improved 1865 model Gatling which came too late for the war. Though even the 1862 version was superior to the Agar Gun, the U.S. Ordnance remained uninterested until General Butler personally ordered twelve (using them at Petersburg), Porter one, and Hancock twelve. Not officially adopted until 1866.

Billinghurst Requa Battery Gun. Officially not a machine-gun, but a volley-gun; 25 barrels, .25 cal. Mounted on two-wheeled carriage, all barrels fired simultaneously, clips of 25 cartridges being inserted at once. Seven volleys per minute with a crew of three; became virtually useless in rain as wet cartridges often misfired; could explode if touched by stray sparks. Used mostly as defence for covered bridges. Range over 1,000 yards.

Vandenberg Volley-Gun. Not a machine-gun; from 85 to 451 barrels, firing musket-balls, the whole enclosed in a single barrel resembling a very thick Howitzer. Mounted on standard artillery carriage. Could be fired in volleys or all barrels discharged in unison. Less successful even than the Billinghurst; vicious recoil and extreme weight rendered the gun unmanageable.

FIREARMS OF THE CIVIL WAR

RIFLES AND CARBINES

As late as 1863 the Union had over 100 models of rifle and carbine listed as official issue weapons; together with the numerous non-regulation patterns used, that figure could well be doubled. The details given below are for the most important firearms used by both sides during the war.

U.S. Percussion Musket, Model 1842. Smoothbore, calibre .69, effective at 100 yards; two to three shots per minute, misfire rate as low as one in 166 shots. About 150,000 used in the Civil War; the standard weapon of the Confederacy until after Gettysburg.

U.S. Rifle, Model 1841 ('Mississippi' or 'Jäger' Rifle). Rifled, cal. .54, modified to .58 upon introduction of the Minié bullet in 1850. Total production 101,096.

Palmetto Muskets. Several patterns copied from the 1841–42 U.S. rifle and musket models manufactured before the war by the Palmetto factory, South Carolina; 6,000 muskets and 1,000 rifles produced 1852–53; no weapons made during the war.

U.S. Rifle Musket, Model 1855. Rifled, cal. .58, using Maynard Tape primer system. About 47,000 produced 1857–61. Reasonably accurate at 500 yards; useless for hitting specific target at longer range.

U.S. Rifle, Model 1855 ('Harper's Ferry' Rifle). Shorter version of the U.S. Rifle Musket, Model 1855.

U.S. Rifle Musket, Model 1861; with two modifications, Models 1863 (1) and 1863 (2). The principal infantry longarm of the war, the Springfield Armoury manufacturing about 800,000, other sources producing 900,000 more. Known as 'Springfield' musket. Confederacy captured about 150,000. Essentially the same as the Model 1855, with the Maynard system (which proved unsatisfactory) replaced by the normal percussion cap. Rifled, cal. .58; maximum range 1,000 yards, effective range 300; rate of fire from three to six shots per minute. Shorter version produced for artillery use. Model 1863 (2) was last U.S. muzzle-loading pattern.

U.S. Musket, Model 1822. Surprisingly, as late as 1862 many Confederates were armed with outdated flintlocks of this (and earlier) patterns. Smoothbore, muzzle-loading, cal. .69; effective range 100 yards or less, rate of fire two to three shots per minute; misfired about one out of six. Virtually useless in wet weather when powder in priming-pan became wet. Shortages in the Confederate army meant that many units were encumbered with these archaic weapons: at Fort Henry, the 10th Tennessee – 'the best equipped regiment in the command' – was armed with Tower flintlocks carried by the local militia in 1812.

Enfield Rifle Musket. After the Springfield, the most numerous weapon in the war; British-made, over 800,000 purchased by both sides. Rifled, cal. .577, muzzle-loading. Considered superior in workmanship and accuracy to Springfield; maximum range 1,100 yards, accurate at 500. Rate of fire two to three rounds per minute.

Remington Rifle Musket. The Remington Arms Co. provided the U.S. with 39,000 Model 1863 rifle muskets.

Brunswick Rifle. Imported from Europe, outdated and 'nearly worthless'. Little improvement (if any) on the flintlock; wildly inaccurate, difficult to load and much prone to fouling.

Whitworth Rifle. English-made precision sniper's arm, used by Confederacy in small numbers (probably less than 100 used). Cal. .451, deadly at 800 yards in trained hands; deviation of only 11½ feet at 1,800 yards. Often fitted with telescopic sight; slow to load and fouled badly.

Sniper rifles. Often privately-owned; heavy and cumbersome, but compared favourably to modern weapons. With telescopic sights, Berdan's U.S. Sharpshooters performed incredible feats with such rifles.

Sharps Rifle. Breech-loading, cal. .52 (also produced in .427 and .373). Only 9,141 purchased by U.S. Government, but many by individuals and State governments. Standard arm of sharpshooter units in later stages of the war. Accurate to 600 yards, but main advantage was rate of fire (up to ten rounds per minute), over three times as fast as muzzle-loaders. Could be loaded from prone position, which was almost impossible with muzzle-loader without causing reduction in rate of fire or causing great inconvenience. Excellent, reliable firearm. Confederacy bought 1,600 in 1861.

'Richmond Sharps' Rifle. Confederate copy of the Sharps; workmanship and performance generally inferior to the original.

Spencer Rifle. Together with the Spencer Carbine, the best breech-loader of the war; 12,000 purchased by U.S. Government. Produced in several calibres; main advantage was the fact that it was a repeater, magazine holding 8 shots. Rate of fire up to 21 rounds per minute, effect of which was quite devastating. Used copper Spencer cartridge; captured Spencer useless to Confederacy when ammunition ran out, as the South had no way of manufacturing these cartridges.

Henry Rifle. U.S. repeater; magazine held 15 shots. Cal. .44; about 10,000 used. Could fire 15 shots in 11 seconds, 120 shots in 5 minutes 54 seconds (including reloading time). Faster than Spencer, but more likely to jam.

Colt Rifle, Model 1855. 5-shot, revolving chamber rifle, cal. .56; unsafe because of possibility of all chambers igniting at once, causing severe explosion; unpopular and replaced as soon as possible.

Hall Rifle, pattern 1811. Strange breech-loading flintlock, cal. .53, though made in other calibres; smoothbore versions also existed, and many converted to muzzle-loaders early in war. Used in small numbers by Confederacy. Little more accurate than ordinary flintlock.

Kerr Rifle. English-made, used in small numbers by Confederacy; cal. .44. Used as sniper's rifle.

Spencer Carbine. Like the Spencer Rifle, the best breechloader in use; more than 94,000 used by Federal troops. Cal. .52; rate of fire as Spencer Rifle. Waterproof; same cartridges as rifle. Best cavalry arm of the war, being the decisive factor in numerous cavalry actions. Effective at 400 yards.

Sharps Carbine. Breech-loader, cal. .52. Over 80,000 purchased by U.S. Government. Range and rate of fire as Sharps Rifle; excellent cavalry weapon, only slightly inferior to Spencer, and then only in rate of fire.

Burnside Carbine. Single-shot percussion weapon, using brass cartridge; cal. .54. Over 55,000 bought by U.S.; effective range 200 yards.

Smith Carbine. Single-shot, percussion, cal. .52; cartridges of brass, paper or rubber. Breech-loading; over 30,000 purchased by U.S.

Maynard Carbine. Breech-loading, percussion, cal. .50. Brass cartridge. 20,202 bought by U.S.

Starr Carbine. Breech-loading, percussion, cal. .54. Linen cartridge. Over 25,000 bought by U.S.

Gallager Carbine. Breech-loading, percussion; cal. .54. Brass or foil and paper cartridge. Over 22,000 bought by U.S.

Joslyn Carbine. Breech-loading, cal. .52; fired Spencer .56–52 cartridge. Over 10,000 bought by U.S.

Remington Carbine. Single-shot, cal. .50, using Spencer cartridge. Used in small numbers in later part of war.

Confederate carbines. Many captured Federal weapons used by Confederate cavalry; British muzzle-loading .577 Enfield Carbine used by both sides early in war and remained popular with Confederacy throughout. Reliable and accurate, though slow in rate of fire when compared to more sophisticated Federal weapons. Other Confederate-manufactured guns included the 'Richmond Sharps', and two muzzle-loading guns, the Murray and Cooke & Brother. Morse single-shot breech-loader firing metal cartridge was produced in small numbers. Confederate cavalrymen seem to have preferred double-barrelled shotguns to carbines, firing both barrels from the saddle into their enemies' faces and then continuing the fusilade with revolvers.

NOTE – in general, carbines were reasonably accurate at 500 yards, but 150–200 was considered effective range.

An interesting sidelight on calculations of accuracy of various firearms concerns the loading drill; inexperienced troops in the heat of battle frequently panicked and fired away their ramrods, making their guns temporarily useless; rammed the cartridges down bullet-first, or continued ramming charge after charge down the barrel in a frenzy of terror. After Gettysburg, of more than 37,000 muskets salvaged, 24,000 were loaded, 18,000 of which had more than one cartridge in the barrel; one gun had 23 loads! From these remarkable figures, it has been calculated that 35 per cent of troops engaged at Gettysburg were ineffective as far as their firearms were concerned!

PISTOLS

About 374,000 revolvers were purchased by the Federal Government; the pistol was a favourite sidearm of Confederate volunteers early in the war, and thousands were purchased privately by both sides. In addition to the principal types noted below, many outmoded flintlocks were used; numerous types could be fitted with shoulderstocks, the 1851 Colt Navy revolver even having a shoulderstock which contained a canteen!

Colt Revolvers. The most famous revolving pistol manufactured in the world, three basic patterns were used during the Civil War. The Model 1848 'Dragoon' was a massive .44 cal. rifled pistol, weighing over four pounds. The two most popular styles – the Model 1851 'Navy' and Model 1860 'Army' – became the favourite sidearm of the South and North respectively. The Navy (cal. .36) was the prototype for many Confederate copies, while the Army (cal. .44) was the principal revolver of the war. The Model 1861 Navy was not as popular, only 2,056 being purchased by the army and hardly any by the navy. Total Federal purchases during the war topped 146,000 (107,156 being of the Army pattern), though the total number in use was probably three times as many: over 200,000 of the 1851 Navy were produced up to 1865. Maximum range was up to 300 yards, but the pistol (in all its many forms) was essentially a close-quarter weapon, effective range being between 25 and 50 yards. All were single-action (the hammer having to be cocked manually before each shot).

Confederate Colt copies. Most 'home-produced' Confederate pistols were copies of various Colt patterns, sometimes including new innovations in mechanism; the principal manufacturers were Griswold & Gunnison, Dance Bros, Leech & Rigden, Rigdon-Ansley, Tucker, Sherrod & Co., Spiller & Burr, and Columbus.

Palmetto pistols. The Palmetto factory of South Carolina produced copies of the Model 1842 single-shot cal. .54 percussion pistol before the war, which were used by the Confederacy.

U.S. Springfield single-shot pistol carbine, percussion, Model 1855. Made obsolete by the more accurate and faster-firing revolver. Equipped with detachable shoulder-stock.

Remington revolvers. The Remington New Model revolver cal. .44, was second in popularity behind the Colt; 125,314 were purchased by the U.S Government during the war. Six-shot, single-action, percussion. Similar in range, etc. to the Colt. The Remington .36 was less popular, being made principally for the U.S. Navy.

Starr revolvers. Next in popularity after the Remington .44, the Federal Government purchased 47,952. Most popular was the Starr Army .44, six-shot, double-action (self-cocking); fired self-consuming cartridge or could be loaded with loose powder and ball. Percussion; single-action model was also produced, as well as a Navy .36 model, the latter much less popular than the .44.

Savage Navy revolver. 11,284 purchased by U.S. Government; cal. .36, equipped with two triggers, one of which revolved cylinder and cocked hammer, the other firing the cartridge.

Whitney revolver. Cal. .36; 11,214 purchased by Federals.

Deane & Adams revolver. English-made, though many manufactured by Massachusetts Arms Co. Army model, cal. .44, five-shot, double-action. Also produced in .36 calibre.

Le Mat revolver. Invented by Dr Le Mat of New Orleans; due to difficulties of supply of raw materials and lack of facilities, Le Mat went to Paris where he produced 3,000 revolvers and a few carbines. Revolver popular in Confederacy; several calibres, .40 and .44 most common. Double-barrelled, nine-shot; upper barrel fired bullets, lower barrel smoothbore, firing cal. .60 shotgun charge, hence nickname of 'Grapeshot pistol'. Most effective, very deadly and very popular; used by Beauregard, J. E. B. Stuart and Anderson.

Lefaucheaux revolver. Made in France and Belgium, various calibres, .41 most popular; U.S. Government bought almost 12,000, also used by Confederacy. Pin-fire.

Wesson & Leavitt revolver. Patented 1837, somewhat outmoded. Hammer on side of pistol; six-shot, made in .40 and .31; cal. .40 most popular.

Other revolvers. Numerous other designs were used in considerable quantities, including Tranter .36 and .44 double-action (British), imported by Confederacy; Butterfield .44 Percussion Army, five-shot; Sharps .32 rimfire, four-barrelled pistol; Rogers & Spencer .44 (purchased by U.S.); Pettingell .44 (purchased by U.S.); Beal (12,251 purchased by U.S.); Joslyn (1,100 purchased by U.S.); Bentley (imported by Confederacy); Kerr (imported by Confederacy); Raphael.

EDGED WEAPONS OF THE CIVIL WAR

SABRES

Officially a cavalry and light artillery weapon, the sabre was accorded nothing like the respect it had in Europe. Apart from such notable actions as Brandy Station, the cavalry on both sides was used more as mounted infantry, having few opportunities to use the sword. Consequently, it was often discarded as being an encumberance, the Confederate cavalry in particular preferring rifles, carbines, and more popularly shotguns and revolvers, sometimes up to four or six of the latter being carried by each man. An additional difficulty was the fact that new recruits had considerable trouble in learning how to use the sabre; in the earlier part of the war one-eared horses were quite common in volunteer regiments! The sabre, however, did have its adherents among the regimental officers and staffs of both armies.

Sabres carried during the war included varying patterns of the curved U.S. army issue, as well as an assortment of European weapons imported by the Confederacy, including a quantity of straight-bladed 'Prussian' sabres. An interesting sidelight on the effectiveness of sabres comes from a Confederate general who wrote that when his infantry were charged by Union cavalry, the Southerners raised the cry: 'Boys, here are those fools coming again with their sabres; give it to them!' Frequently, Confederates were *compelled* to fight as mounted infantry from the single fact that they had no sabres – Logan's Brigade in October 1864 is an example of a 'sabreless' cavalry command.

SWORDS

Officially carried by officers, senior N.C.O.s and musicians, swords were generally restricted to those of commissioned rank, the lower ranks finding the sword an unnecessary piece of equipment. Generally, the sword was a symbol of rank rather than a useful weapon: the short artillery sword was almost totally useless for everything except chopping firewood.

BAYONETS

Issued to almost all infantrymen in the war, the bayonet (generally of 'socket' pattern, though a number of 'sword-bayonets' were issued to Zouave and similar units) was most useful as a roasting spit, can opener, entrenching tool – in fact anything except as a weapon. Though there were a large number of heroic 'charges' during the war (often executed at a slow pace), the contest was almost invariably settled by a close-range fire-fight before the combatants could come within hand-to-hand range. Few actual bayonet-fights occurred, those which did being carefully recorded as exceptionally unusual events: the charge of the 17th Wisconsin at Corinth, Mississippi, 3 October 1862, for example. Official casualty figures show the ineffectiveness of the bayonet as anything but a morale-booster even more clearly: in Grant's Wilderness campaign, only six of the 7,302 wounded were injured by bayonet or sword; of approximately 250,000 wounded treated in Union hospitals during the war, only 922 bore wounds inflicted by bayonet or sword, a large percentage of which occurred as the result of private quarrels or brawls in camp.

LANCES

Another important cavalry weapon in Europe was almost totally neglected in the Civil War. The 6th Pennsylvania Cavalry (Rush's Lancers) were armed with lances for a time, until it was realised that the weapon was totally unsuited for the type of warfare in which they were engaged. The 26th Texas Cavalry may have been armed with lances, and other corps bore the name 'Lancers' – for example, the Kelley Lancers (1st West Virginia Cavalry), The United States Lancers (The Westfield Cavalry [part of the 9th New York Cavalry]), and Lucas Sobolaski's Independent Company of Lancers (Missouri). The Americans were the first to realise that the day of the lance as a cavalry weapon was over – some European nations persisted with it for more than fifty years after.

KNIVES

Known by the generic term 'Bowie knife' (though few actually resembled the original designed by Colonel James Bowie of Alamo fame), all manner of fighting knives were carried at the outbreak of war, principally by Confederate volunteers. Indeed, some of the early portrait photographs would lead one to believe that the knife was the only weapon, so prominently were they displayed! The heavy knives were of limited value and most went the same way as all other pieces of non-essential equipment – thrown down by the roadside on the line of march.

PIKES

Apart from a brief resurrection as the principal arm of the ill-equipped Prussian militia in 1813, the pike had been abandoned as archaic by even the most backward European nations two hundred years prior to the Civil War, yet – incredibly – there were members of the Confederate War Department who pressed for the introduction of whole regiments of pikemen. In 1862, twenty such regiments were planned, and in April of the same year it was authorised that every Confederate regiment should include two companies of pikemen: even Lee fell in with this insane plan. Large numbers of pikes were produced at considerable expense and waste of time and materials, but fortunately for those intended to be armed with pikes, the plan was never put into effect.

REGIMENTAL UNIFORMS

The following brief descriptions concern regimental and departmental uniforms of corps not illustrated; they are miscellaneous examples of the type of dress worn by whole regiments which did not conform to official regulations.

UNION ARMY

3rd New York Wore grey militia uniforms early in the war.

6th New York (Wilson's Zouaves) This notably inefficient regiment wore grey jackets of 'shoddy' furnished by the State.

10th New York (National Zouaves) Originally wore dark brown Zouave uniforms with red trimming; received new uniform in October 1861 consisting of dark brown jackets trimmed red, red waistcoats, light blue trousers trimmed red, fez, and white canvas leggings. Uniform fitted 'easily but yet not too loosely'.

11th New York (Ellsworth's 1st Fire Zouaves) Originally wore red képi, blue Zouave jacket with yellow trimming, loose red trousers tucked into leather leggings, and 'high shoes'. Soon after commencement of war adopted a grey jacket with blue facings and red lace, red shirts, red cap with blue band, trousers red or grey with red stripe, tan calfskin gaiters.

12th New York On 8 May 1861 received a handsome 'Chasseur' uniform consisting of long dark blue coats, light blue baggy trousers, and a 'modified fatigue cap'.

13th New York At First Bull Run wore uniforms of appalling quality, 'hastily ordered and hastily made' by an unscrupulous contractor; the dull grey 'shoddy' uniforms were dubbed 'Penitentiary Uniforms'. Many of the men 'were dressed only in shirts and drawers' – 'a ragged mob', as the uniforms fell apart after a few hours wear.

14th New York Wore French-style 'cutaway' shell-jackets and white baggy trousers at First Bull Run.

16th New York Wore straw hats in the Peninsular Campaign.

20th New York For some time after first muster in April 1861, wore soft, light-coloured 'Hardee' hats.

31st New York This regiment had several Polish Companies; the men wore 'Polish quadrangular caps of red and white' (these might possibly have been of the czapka (lancer-cap) style, but are more likely to have resembled the lower-crowned 'Konfedratka').

40th New York (Mozart Regiment) Many of its members coming from Massachusetts, the regiment left for the front in Massachusetts grey uniforms, including double-breasted frock-coats. These uniforms were ordered to be returned to Massachusetts, but probably were sold to New York second-hand clothing dealers! The regiment had overcoats of heavy black material, trimmed with red; these were later replaced by the regulation light blue.

44th New York (Ellsworth's Avengers) Officers and N.C.O.s wore regulation infantry uniform; the privates had a Zouave-style costume, consisting of blue képi, blue jackets with red trim and brass buttons, red shirts with yellow trim, blue trousers with red stripes, yellow leggings and linen havelocks. Soon replaced by regulation uniform.

54th New York ('Schwarzer Jäger') Consisted exclusively of Germans, recruited in 1861 as the Schwarzer Jäger ('Black Rifles'), copied from the famous Prussian unit, Lützow's 'Black Corps'. Uniformed in black with silver trimming.

55th New York (Gardes Lafayette) Wore French-style uniforms; red képi, and light blue coat with black braid on the sleeves.

62nd New York (Anderson's Zouaves) In October 1861 this regiment was the most sloppy, unclean and generally disgraceful regiment in Union service. The gaudy Zouave costume always attracted a rowdy element (as in Wheat's Louisiana 'Tigers'), but this corps contained nothing but vagabonds who stole from friend, foe and civilian alike. The camps of this corps were permanently covered with rubbish and filth.

69th New York (Meagher's Zouaves) Dark blue Zouave cap and jacket with red braid; light blue shirt, sash and trousers, tan gaiters. Officers probably wore regulation infantry uniform; the whole corps later adopted regulation dress.

65th New York (1st U.S. Chasseurs) Details lacking; regiment wore a 'natty uniform' of chasseur pattern.

128th New York Wore regulation dress of 'sickly blue', probably due to bad dye, being much paler than the regulation colour.

140th New York Wore a Zouave costume similar to the 5th New York.

146th New York (Halleck Infantry) On 3 June 1863 the 146th received Zouave uniforms consisting of red fez with red tassel, baggy blue trousers, red sash ten feet long, and white cloth knee-length leggings, the remainder apparently being of the regulation pattern. Also issued with white turbans to be worn around the fez in full dress, which was difficult to put on: 'after much perspiring and considerable profanity, the entire regiment looked not unlike the soldiers of Mahomet'.

165th New York (2nd Duryée Zouaves) Similar in style to that of the original Duryée Zouaves; wore braided Zouave jackets, shirts, Zouave cap and scarlet trousers.

8th New York National Guard Similar uniform to that of the 7th National Guard, but photographs show Mexican-War style caps with large, flat tops in use.

1st New York Marine Artillery Similar uniform to that of the navy; officers wore double-breasted frock-coats and cap with a gold band; no sash, but red shoulder-bars bearing crossed anchor and cannon-barrel in silver embroidery. Other ranks wore naval uniform of dark blue. Infantry detachment was issued with short Belgian rifles and sword-bayonets, while the detachment which worked howitzers had pistols and cutlasses.

22nd Pennsylvania Wore blue militia uniforms early in the war.

23rd Pennsylvania (Birney Zouaves) Wore a handsome dark blue Zouave uniform for first six months of its service; when that wore out, dark blue uniform with brass shoulder-scales was issued, most unpopular with the men after their previous comfortable dress.

72nd Pennsylvania (Baxter's Philadelphia Fire Zouaves) Zouave dress, 'not nearly as showy and foreign as that of the New York Zouaves', consisting of képi, cut-away jacket with rows of 'bright bell buttons' held by a hook and eye at the throat, blue shirt, often with the company letter embroidered on the chest, light blue trousers with red cord at the sides, and white leggings, the latter unpopular with the men for being too conspicuous on the skirmish-line and at night.

88th Pennsylvania Company 'B' tried to imitate the 'Bucktails' by wearing squirrel-tails in their headgear; this greatly displeased the Colonel, who ordered them removed immediately.

155th Pennsylvania Magnificent Zouave costume much liked by the men, but with one drawback – it enabled stragglers to be identified too easily. Heavy dark blue jacket with yellow trim on collar, cuffs, and breast; wide, dark blue knee-breeches; red flannel sash trimmed with yellow, ten feet long by one foot wide; white canvas leggings; and turban 'of Turkish model' composed of a piece of white flannel the same size as the sash, replaced by a red fez with tassel on all but full-dress occasions.

5th Massachusetts In the early months of the war had black overcoats of 'shoddy', the dye of which ran into their uniforms at the slightest shower of rain. As the regiment marched down State Street in Boston on their way to the transport ship, the whole corps dumped their overcoats in the street by way of protest. They soon received regulation issue coats.

8th Massachusetts (Salem Zouaves) Wore modified Zouave dress, consisting of red képi, dark blue jacket and trousers trimmed with scarlet braid, and white leggings.

13th Massachusetts Wore blue militia-style uniforms.

22nd Massachusetts On 2 September 1862 at the end of the Peninsular Campaign, described as dressed in rags, with straw hats and 'slouch' hats, many with no socks, some completely barefoot: this was the typical condition of any regiment after a few months hard campaigning without a replacement of uniform.

23rd Massachusetts Wore Zouave jackets of grey flannel faced blue, dark blue trousers and grey cap, all trimmed with red; officers had single-breasted grey frock-coats with blue collars and cuffs, dark blue trousers, and blue képis, the cap and coat trimmed with gold braid. The uniform was replaced by regulation fatigue dress after some members of Company 'A' had been seen stealing turkeys: the Colonel turned in the distinctive uniforms because he did not want his men to be so easily identified on their next 'foraging expedition'!

1st Battalion, Massachusetts Rifles In April 1861 wore a dark green uniform trimmed with light green.

Boston Rifle Company On 12 May 1861 wore fatigue cap, light blue trousers, red shirt and dark grey overcoat. Armed with Whitney rifles and sword-bayonet.

Massachusetts Independent Corps of Cadets From 1861 to 1864 wore grey uniforms trimmed red, and leather shakos with red pompom and red and white rosette. In full dress wore black chapeau with red plume; a blue uniform was worn in the field.

4th Connecticut Wore very uncomfortable uniforms in 1861, consisting of short coats without skirts and trousers of thick grey woollen material 'made, one would have thought, especially for midwinter wear in Greenland', with matching heavy grey felt hats. The uniforms were ill-cut: coats were too big, trouser-waists too wide, some trousers three inches too long and others the same length too short. Shirts were of heavy, grey coarse flannel.

New Haven Greys Wore typical volunteer uniform in 1859: blue frock coats with red shoulder knots and blue pants, 'all richly finished in gilt and braid, a very striking and handsome uniform'.

1st Vermont Wore grey militia-style uniforms in early months of war.

3rd New Hampshire Wore helmets in early part of service, these being shaped like tropical pith helmets.

Indiana Regiments Of the first six Indiana regiments in 1861, only the Wallace Zouaves wore a uniform of its own design; the other five apparently wore grey or blue jackets and trousers and 'Hardee' hat.

1st Rhode Island Rifles Apparently wore 'hunting shirts' or 'Rhode Island' blouses in 1861, of blue or leather colour, with 'Hardee' hat.

1st Rhode Island Light Artillery Judging from a photograph of a regimental chaplain, the corps wore 'Rhode Island' blouses of dark blue. Light Artillery dress shakos were issued but worn only briefly.

1st Iowa Wore grey militia-style uniform early in war; the neckerchief worn by E. F. Ware of Company 'E' provides an example of non-regulation dress. He purchased this item for 50 cents in Boonville, Missouri, in 1861, and used it as a neckerchief, necktie and havelock. It was a large, red-bordered cotton square, with a printed picture in the centre of a large blue steamboat on a yellow river!

Ellet's Mississippi Marine Brigade Comprising 10 companies of infantry, four of cavalry and a 6-gun light artillery battery, the corps operated Federal gunboats and kept river-banks clear of Confederate guerrillas attempting to fire on Union boats. Wore regulation uniform, but the caps were made 'with full, round tops, broad straight visors', and had a green band trimmed with gold lace.

Telegraphers Officially Telegraph Corps operators were civilian personnel, but General G. H. Thomas ordered that as from 26 March 1864 all telegraph operators in his Department of the Cumberland were to wear officers' képis without badges, dark blue fatigue-blouses with Staff buttons, and dark blue trousers with a one-eighth inch silver stripe on the outer seams. This led to some embarrassment and much amusement as operators were frequently mistaken for staff colonels and even generals! Many reverted to their former civilian dress, though some wore uniform until the end of the war. On 5 July 1864 a similar dress regulation was issued for telegraphers of the Department of the Tennessee, except that it also included a small silver cord around the cap-band.

Balloon Corps Balloon-observers were civilian employees and as such wore no uniform, though some sported unofficial hat badges of the letters 'B.C.' (Balloon Corps) or 'A.D.' (Aeronautic Department) which usually provoked so much ridicule that they were quickly discarded!

Chaplains Regimental chaplains were authorised (on 25 November 1861) to wear black felt hat or képi without ornament, double-breasted black frock-coat with nine buttons, and black trousers, with a plain black chapeau worn in full dress. On 25 August 1864 black coat-braid and the Staff hat-badge were authorised, the former to be worn around the button-holes. Many chaplains, however, adopted regimental uniform of captain, complete with sash, shoulder-bars, sword and often pistol; Chaplain Winslow of the 5th New York, for example, wore Zouave officer's uniform. The chaplain of the 34th Massachusetts asked the colonel to publish a regimental order allowing him to wear captain's shoulder-bars, as his pay was equal to that of a captain, and only by wearing shoulder-bars was he allowed to purchase whiskey!

Provost-Marshals To wear uniform of a captain of General Staff when engaged on such duties.

Officers of the Day To wear regimental uniform with the sash not worn around the waist, but across the body from the right shoulder, the tassels on the left hip.

Signal Officers To wear uniform of a Major of General Staff (General Order 15 June 1861).

Military Storekeeper To wear civilian frock-coat of blue, with buttons of the unit to which attached; round black hat, white or dark blue trousers and waistcoat, black cravat.

Marine Corps In full dress, Field Officers wore a chapeau with red feather plume, company officers and other ranks having leather shakos with red pompom and brass plate, the latter bearing the marine badge of the infantry hunting-horn with the letter 'M' in the ring. Officers wore epaulettes on their frock-coats with insignia of rank as worn by the army; all ranks wore the frock-coat for service ashore, with white cross-belts; ordinary fatigue uniforms including blue képi with the Marine hunting-horn in brass were the most common form of dress on active service. In full dress, senior N.C.O.s (Sergeant-Major, Quartermaster-Sergeant, Drum-Major and Chief Musicians) had double-breasted dark blue frock-coats with two rows of seven buttons, two loops of yellow lace with buttons on each side of the collar; collars edged red (Drum-Major's and Chief Musicians' edged white); round cuffs with slashes, each slash having three small loops of yellow lace and buttons, edged red (white for Drum-Major and Chief Musicians); rear pockets edged red (or white). Drum-Majors and Chief Musicians had frock-coats of scarlet; all coats were lined black. Other ranks wore two loops of lace on the cuffs; Musicians wore frock-coats like the privates, but of scarlet with white piping like those of the Drum-Major and Chief Musicians. Marine Corps chevrons were of yellow lace, worn points up

130

(unlike those of the army): Sergeant-Major, three chevrons and an arc on a scarlet patch; Quartermaster-Sergeant, three chevrons and a 'tie' on a scarlet patch; Drum-Major like the Quartermaster-Sergeant, but with a white star in the centre, on a scarlet patch; other ranks wore army-style chevrons, of yellow lace, points up.

CONFEDERATE ARMY

South Carolina The Volunteer companies of this state wore a wider range of uniforms than perhaps any other; British war correspondent William H. Russell wrote on 12 April 1861: 'There is an endless variety – often of ugliness – in dress and equipment and nomenclature among these companies . . . the tunic is of different cuts, colours, facings and materials – green with grey and yellow, grey with orange and black and white, blue with white and yellow facings, roan brown, burnt sienna and olive – jackets, frocks, tunics, blouses, cloth, linen, tweed, flannel'. Head-dress were generally of some type of képi, though straw and felt hats were common, while 'some men wore leather helmets, either the crested dragoon type or the Prussian spike type'. It is interesting to learn that some of these leather helmets 'probably dated back to the War of 1812 era', which does not rule out the possibility of their being of the British fur-crested 'Tarleton' pattern; whilst others wore more modern 'pickelhaube' spiked helmets. 'Corsican' caps were also used, these being peaked cloth forage caps with a hanging bag and tassel at one side. An early South Carolina uniform was described as being worn by officers in Charleston in mid-April 1861; these consisted of blue képis with Palmetto tree badges, blue coats with standing collars, shoulder-straps, gilt buttons bearing the Palmetto in relief, and blue trousers with gold lace cord stripes. Officers of the U.S. Army who changed their allegiance upon secession wore their U.S. uniforms until they wore out or until they could obtain new grey ones; many South Carolinans wore U.S. blue for several months after the outbreak of war. States like North Carolina and Georgia also wore blue uniforms in early 1861, like Federal costume but with state insignia.

14th Virginia Cavalry Company 'H' (Rockbridge Dragoons) wore leather helmets, probably of 1812 vintage, in the early stages of the war.

Citadel Cadets (South Carolina Volunteers) This Charleston-raised company wore black shakos with brass plates and white plumes, grey frock-coats with black collars and cuff-lace, grey trousers with black stripes, and white or black leather equipment.

6th Virginia The Elliott Greys (Company 'I') wore (according to a photograph of a drummer) a tasselled Zouave-cap, grey cut-away coat with dark shoulder-straps and three rows of buttons, dark trousers and white gaiters.

1st Alabama In Montgomery, Alabama, the 1st Alabama was issued with enamelled cloth knapsacks and cedar barrel-canteens in March 1862; otherwise the men provided their own 'uniforms', of which no two were alike!

Alabama Volunteer Cadets At Alexandria, Virginia in 1861 (September) this company wore caps decorated with the letters 'A.V.C.'.

20th Tennessee Composed of Tennessee farm boys, wore several styles of plain grey shell-jacket and trousers, with black hats and equipment; originally armed with 1812 flintlocks, later with Enfields.

North Carolina Militia May have been one of the units to wear fatigue uniforms of 'butternut' even before the war.

4th Georgia Company 'B' (La Grange Light Guards) wore pre-war militia style uniforms; for officers, grey frock-coat with black collar and black edging to pointed cuffs, black shoulder-bars edged gold; black képi; grey trousers with black stripe, red sash, black belts with brass plates bearing Georgia state seal.

Indians The various Indian regiments (composed mainly of full-blood and half-breed Cherokees, Chickasaws, Choctaws and Creeks with some Osages and Seminoles) were issued (when available) with standard Confederate grey shell-jackets and 'slouch' hats, but many wore Indian trousers, moccasins, and shirts of buckskin or trade-cloth; a large number were virtually indistinguishable from 'wild' Indians. The Cherokee Mounted Rifles had grey jackets with yellow facings. Arms were an assortment of Confederate, captured Union and civilian weapons together with native items like lances, bows and arrows, tomahawks and knives. Union Indians (Creeks, Cherokees, Osages with some Senecas, Delawares and Tuscaroras) wore Federal fatigue dress, with some native items.

Marines No regulations are known to exist of the Confederate Marine Corps uniform; it is possible that they were copied from those of the U.S. Marines, with grey substituted for blue, but it is likely that many individual variations existed. Officers wore grey frock-coats, usually double-breasted, with rank indicated by shoulder-bars or sleeve-lace; it is known that double-breasted frock-coats with turndown collars of

132

blue or black material also existed. Képis were worn in different weights of cloth for summer and winter; trousers were blue or grey. Other ranks wore képis or felt hats like the army; shirts were blue flannel, and trousers sky blue like those of the U.S. Marines. Grey jackets were probably worn also. On 6 May 1861 Captain A. C. van Benthuysen's Marine company at Pensacola, Florida, wore blue pants and grey flannel shirts; later in 1861 they received white pants, blue flannel shirts and white 'jumpers'. These items were probably intended as a temporary dress until regulation items could be issued.

Prisoners of War The United States Government provided thousands of uniforms for Confederate prisoners, these conforming to Confederate regulations in every way except for the buttons. Thus many 'exchanged' prisoners rejoined the Confederate army wearing uniforms supplied by the Union!

Guerrillas and 'Bushwhackers' Confederate guerrillas sometimes wore items of regulation dress, but were more often dressed as civilians. The following is a contemporary description of a 'bushwhacker' seen in Virginia in 1862:

'. . . a stolid, vicious-looking countenance, an ungainly figure in a garb of the coarsest texture of homespun linen or linsey-woolsey, tattered and torn, and so covered with dirt as not to enable one to guess its original colour; a dilapidated, rimless hat or cap of some wild animal covering his head, which has not been combed for months; his feet covered with moccasins, and a rifle by his side, a powder horn and a shot-pouch slung around his neck . . .'

Fig. 1. Shako, 7th New York Militia; black felt with black leather reinforcements, gilt plates; white plume.

Fig. 2. U.S. Infantry musician's shako.

Fig. 3. Confederate 'Corsican cap'.

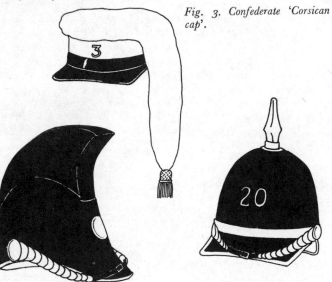

Fig. 4. Confederate cavalry helmet; black leather, antiquated pattern.

Fig. 5. Confederate volunteer helmet; styled after the Prussian 'pickelhaube'.

HEAD-DRESS (from contemporary illustrations).

1. U.S.A.: Major-General, Full Dress.

In full dress, General Officers wore the regulation double-breasted frock-coat, with collar and cuffs of black or very dark blue velvet. Rank was denoted by the arrangement of the buttons: Brigadier-Generals had buttons in groups of two, eight per row; Major-Generals in threes, nine in each row; and Lieutenant-Generals in fives, ten in each row. Rank was also indicated by the badge on the gold lace epaulettes – one silver star for Brigadier-Generals, two for Major-Generals, and three for Lieutenant-Generals. The badge on the felt hat consisted of the letters 'u.s.' in silver embroidery, surrounded by a gold-embroidered laurel wreath; as an alternative to the felt hat, General Officers were authorised to wear a low-crowned black bicorn in full dress, with gold lace decoration; in practice it seems to have been used only rarely. In design it resembled that worn by the Confederate army (illustrated in Plate 34).

The buff silk waist-sash was a further distinction of rank, as was the ornate shabraque, bearing rank insignia in the form of stars in the rear corners. Laced holster-caps to match the shabraque were sometimes used, though many preferred plain black leather designs. Swords were carried by all General Officers in full dress; the regulation pattern (Model 1860) had a thin, light blade, often replaced by a more sturdy version for active service.

2. U.S.A.: Brigadier-Generals, Service Dress.

Both figures on this plate are taken from original photographs, and show how the personal whim of individual officers led to numerous non-regulation styles being worn on active service. The black felt hat could be 'punched up' in the crown to resemble a dunce's cap, which style, though appearing slightly ridiculous, was favoured by General Burnside and extensively copied by his staff. The more usual method of wearing the hat (as shown on the other figure) resembled the full dress style. General McDowell wore a pith helmet as a protection from the sun; it was described as 'like an inverted washbowl'.

Regulation undress uniform consisted of a plain dark blue frock-coat, double-breasted with buttons arranged according to rank as in full dress, with a standing collar; and plain dark blue trousers. In this plate are illustrated two versions, one longer and one shorter than the regulation, both with turned-down collars and one with cut lapels, both revealing the shirt-collar. This type of garment was often worn without rank-bars; indeed, even Ulysses Grant was described on various occasions as being almost indistinguishable from a Union private or even a civilian! Just before Antietam, Burnside was thus described:

'dressed so as to be almost unrecognizable as a general officer; wore a rough blouse on the collar of which a close look revealed two much-battered and faded stars, indicating his rank . . . he wore a black 'Slouch' hat, the brim well down over his face.'

3. U.S.A.: a) 1st Lieutenant,

Cavalry, Service Dress.
b) Private, Cavalry, Service Dress.
c) Corporal, 2nd Cavalry, Full Dress, 1860–61.

When the U.S. Cavalry was re-organised in 1861, the two dragoon regiments became the 1st and 2nd Cavalry. Prior to this reorganisation, they had been distinguished by orange braid and trimming, which was changed to the cavalry distinctive colour (yellow); for a time, however, it appears that the old dragoon trim was retained.

The black felt hat, standard issue for all branches of the army in full dress, was known as the 'Hardee', 'Kossuth' or 'Jeff Davis' pattern; it had a yellow hatcord and black plume, the latter reserved for parade. On the front was a brass crossed sabres badge with regimental number and company identification letter; the turned-up brim was secured by a brass badge consisting of the U.S. eagle and shield device. A variation on the 'Hardee' pattern was the 'Burnside' hat, basically a lower-crowned replica.

In full dress, the regulation shell-jacket with yellow piping was worn, with two loops of lace at either side of the collar. One such loop was the official distinction of volunteer regiments, but it appears that the 2nd Cavalry (though a regular regiment) also wore one lace. The shoulder-scales and white gloves were reserved for parade. The official Regulations specified dark blue trousers for all branches of the army except Light Artillery, but General Orders of 16 December 1861 authorised the more familiar sky-blue trousers, very few of the dark blue being issued. Equipment was of black leather with brass fittings; the Model 1860 light cavalry sabre was the regulation arm, but some units retained the Model 1840 Dragoon sabre, the only basic difference between the two being the shape of the hand-grip and a slight variation in length.

The most common uniform worn on campaign consisted of the cloth képi and standard pattern fatigue-blouse, occasionally worn with yellow braid trimming. The light blue trousers (few of the dark blue pattern were in evidence) could be worn either inside or outside the boots. The crossed sabres badge officially worn on the front of the képi was often transferred to the top, to allow the cap to be worn in the fashionable 'pressed-down' style; as the war progressed, képi-badges were often abandoned entirely. All manner of non-regulation styles were common on active service, battered full dress hats or other black felt 'slouch' hats being extremely popular.

4. U.S.A.: a) 1st Sergeant, Cavalry, with Sheridan's Guidon.
b) Captain, Cavalry, Full Dress.

Cavalry officers' full dress uniform included the 'Hardee' hat with two feather plumes and cords of mixed black and gold. The hat-badge was embroidered in gold on a black velvet oval, consisting of crossed sabres, with regimental number and company letter for company officers (i.e. up to and including the rank of Captain), and just the regimental number for regimental officers (i.e. Major and upwards). A design of the crossed sabres alone also existed.

In full dress, all officers wore the frock-coat, this garment being single-breasted with nine buttons for company officers, and double-breasted with two rows of seven buttons for regimental officers. The epaulettes worn in full dress were of gold lace with bullion fringes for all except 2nd Lieutenants, whose epaulettes had thin cord fringes. On the epaulette-strap was a silver circle bearing the regimental number (nearest the 'crescent'), and higher up the badges of rank corresponding to those worn on the shoulder-bars of ordinary dress. Trousers were sky blue (though dark blue was the original regulation), with a ⅛th-inch welt on the outer seam. The sabre could be hooked on-to the belt by the upper hanging-ring of the scabbard, allowing the wearer to walk with ease without the necessity of carrying the sword in one hand. Sword-knots were mixed gold and black for officers and black leather for other ranks.

The 1st Sergeant illustrated wears a more or less standard campaign dress (the waistbelt being worn under the fatigue jacket); he carries the personal flag of Major-General Philip H. Sheridan, Cavalry Corps, Army of the Potomac (1865) who, like other cavalry leaders, signified his position in the field by his own unique guidon.

Federal cavalry formations did not possess Corps badges as did their in-fantry counterparts, but two corps had similar badges, worn on the hat or képi. Sheridan's Cavalry corps had a badge consisting of a white sun-burst (the rays having squared-off ends), with a dark blue oval centre bearing yellow crossed sabres (this badge can be seen on the front of the 1st Sergeant's képi). Wilson's Cavalry Corps had a badge consisting of a horizontal yellow carbine, from which hung vertically a red swallow-tailed guidon, suspended from the carbine by two yellow cords, and bearing yellow crossed sabres on the centre of the guidon.

5. U.S.A.: a) Sergeant, Cavalry with Custer's Guidon.
b) Officer, 1st Rhode Island Cavalry.

The Sergeant illustrated in this plate wears the regulation full dress shell-jacket, often worn on campaign with the képi. The trousers had 1½-inch yellow stripes on the outer seams for sergeants. The flag carried is typical of the type carried by orderlies of noted cavalry generals, intended to mark their position on the battle-field: Federal generals Sheridan, Kilpatrick, Merritt and Custer all had 'personal' standards or guidons, that illustrated being the third pattern used by General G. A. Custer. Custer's first flag was a red over blue guidon bearing a crossed sabres badge and two battle honours, the second a more elaborate version with fringe and additional honours, the third that illustrated (bearing the crossed sabres badge in white), and the fourth and final pattern a larger version of the third, with a white tape edge. The flag illustrated was used from June 1864 until March 1865, when Custer commanded the 3rd Cavalry Division. Of all the generals produced by the war, George Armstrong Custer is undoubtedly the most famous, though ironically not for his dashing conduct during the war, nor even his eccentric and ostentateous costume, but for the fact that he and his command fell victim to an Indian ambush which resulted in the 'massacre' of the Little Big Horn in 1876.

The figure of the officer of the 1st Rhode Island Cavalry is taken from a photograph of Colonel Alfred Nattie Duffié. Though conforming to the basic regulation style, unusual features included in the uniform are the double-breasted shell jacket with yellow piping and very 'full' sleeves, and the 'baggy' trousers, the whole ensemble appearing much more French than American. That is hardly surprising, as Duffié was a graduate of the St Cyr military academy and fought with great distinction with the French cavalry in Algiers, Senegal and the Crimea. He further distinguished himself when he emigrated to the United States, rising from his commission as Captain in the 2nd New York Cavalry, to command the 1st Rhode Island Cavalry, to Brigadier-General and divisional commander, becoming an outstanding cavalry commander in the Union army.

6. U.S.A.: a) Private, Cavalry, in 'gum blanket'.

b) Corporal, Cavalry, with Regimental Standard.

The sky blue cavalry overcoat was double-breasted, with a 'stand-and-fall' collar; the cape, lined yellow, could be thrown back over the shoulder. When worn buttoned, the cape extended to the cuff of the great-coat.

Each cavalry regiment carried a Regimental Standard, similar in design to the infantry version but only two feet five inches long by two feet three inches on the pole. The blue ground of the standard bore the design of an eagle with wings outspread, with a red, white and blue U.S. shield on its breast, holding a branch of laurel and a sheaf of arrows in its talons; above the eagle was a scroll inscribed 'E PLURIBUS UNUM' in black lettering, and below a similar scroll bearing the title of the regiment. The standard-bearer illustrated wears the black leather standard-belt over the coat, but under the cape, as was usual for all equipment.

The waterproof 'gum blanket' as shown on the other figure could serve as a 'poncho'-style garment, or (by means of eyelet holes in the corners) be rigged as a one-man 'pup' tent. One of the most useful pieces of equipment issued during the war, it was carried rolled around the blanket or strapped onto the knapsack.

7. U.S.A.: a) Corporal, Cavalry, with Company Guidon.

b) Private, Cavalry, with Designating

Flag, Cavalry Reserve Headquarters, Army of the Potomac, 1862.

Both figures in this plate are shown in campaign dress, being the basic regulation fatigue dress, but with a number of less official details: the corporal, for example, wears the collar of the fatigue-blouse turned down with a coloured neckerchief under the collar, and the common 'slouch' hat.

Each Federal Corps, Division and Brigade had its own 'Designating Flag' intended to mark the position of the headquarters of the formation at all times. Designating flags were made in a variety of sizes and an even larger variety of designs. That illustrated is the Designating Flag of the Cavalry Reserve Headquarters, Army of the Potomac, which was authorised by a General Order of March 1862. The two brigades of the Cavalry Reserve were assigned flags at the same time, these also being yellow, with a five-pointed blue star in the centre for the 1st Brigade, and two similar stars on the flag of the 2nd.

The corporal is shown carrying a Company Guidon of the pattern used until 1863 and after 1865, consisting of a swallow-tailed flag, the red top bearing the white letters 'u.s.' and the white lower portion the company identifying letter. The flag was flown from a nine-feet long pole, topped by the standard brass heart-shaped pike-head. Between 1863 and 1865 a different pattern of guidon was carried by cavalry companies, of the same shape but consisting of a 'stars and stripes' design like that of the National Flag.

8. U.S.A.: Corporal 6th Pennsylvania Cavalry (Rush's Lancers).

Raised as the 70th Volunteers, the 6th Pennsylvania Cavalry (Rush's Lancers) were named after their Colonel, Richard H. Rush. One of the best Federal cavalry regiments, their many battle-honours included Gaines' Mill, Antietam, Fredericksburg, Brandy Station (where they charged and fought continuously for twelve hours) and Gettysburg. The uniform was basically of the regulation style, with dark blue trousers being worn early in the regiment's existence; a photograph taken at Falmouth, Virginia, in 1862 shows them to have been replaced by the more conventional light blue. The regiment wore one loop of lace on the collar (the distinguishing mark of volunteer cavalry); the brass shoulder-scales were soon discarded. Officers wore the crossed sabres badge on the front of the képi, the other ranks having theirs on the crown. On the carbine-belt was worn an unusual brass oval-shaped plate with pointed ends, bearing the device of crossed lances crudely-stamped into the metal.

The regiment took its name from their principal arm: nine-feet long lances of Norwegian fir, with eleven-inch three-sided heads and swallow-tailed pennons. These pennons, supposedly made by the ladies of Philadelphia for the regiment, were of crimson bunting with a binding of scarlet braid. Finally being accepted as unserviceable in May 1863, the lances were replaced by sabres and carbines, though a number of these had been used at the same time as the lances, twelve carbines per troop being issued prior to May 1863.

The plate shows the typical saddle-equipment used by all branches of the Federal cavalry. The leather-covered wooden McClellan saddle was held in place by a girth and surcingle of blue webbing. Stirrups were wooden, covered with leather and including large leather 'hoods' which all but covered the rider's foot. Horse-furniture was generally of black leather with brass fittings and steel bit; the blanket under the saddle was often dark blue with a broad orange stripe near the edge, with 'u.s.' in orange letters at the centre, though grey blankets with yellow trim were not uncommon. On the saddle was carried a canvas nosebag, rolled over-coat, blanket, two black leather saddlebags containing rations, ammunition, clothing, horseshoes and other equipment, and a thirty-feet long lariat.

9. U.S.A.: a) Officer, 3rd Pennsylvania Cavalry (60th Volunteers).
b) Officer, 4th Pennsylvania Cavalry (64th Volunteers).

This plate illustrates two of the typical unorthodox uniforms adopted by officers on campaign: they are taken from photographs of the staffs of Colonel W. W. Averell of the 3rd

Pennsylvania Cavalry (Young's Kentucky Light Cavalry – 60th Volunteers), and of Colonel J. E. Childe of the 4th Pennsylvania Cavalry (64th Volunteers).

The officer of the 3rd wears a half-military, half-civilian costume, only the dark blue jacket indicating to which army he belongs. Even in this case, no badges of rank are worn, and the civilian hat and bow-tie appear somewhat incongruous when coupled with the sabre and pistol.

The officer of the 4th wears a regulation hat, battered almost beyond recognition, and a long blue coat with breast-pocket (from which a handkerchief protrudes), gauntlets, striped shirt and white collar. Both original photographs from which this plate is taken include other officers dressed in more regulation styles, with képis and shell-jackets, though another officer of the 4th wears the same type of long coat, over a dark waistcoat, white shirt and collar, and large dark bow-tie.

10. U.S.A.: a) Private, 3rd New Jersey Cavalry.
b) Private, Benton Hussars.

In the uniform of the 3rd New Jersey Cavalry (1st U.S. Hussars) could be seen the French influence which affected many uniforms during the Civil War. Also known as the Trenton Hussars, the 3rd New Jersey wore the braided dolman-style jacket and 'pillbox' hat so typical of European Hussar regiments. Their attempt at copying these European élite cavalry was hardly an outstanding success –

contemptuously known as 'The Butterflies' because of their uniform, the regiment's reputation in action was equally poor. Forming part of the Army of the Potomac's Cavalry Corps (3rd Brigade, 1st Division), the regiment retreated in haste when under artillery fire at Yellow Tavern (11 May 1864). The excuse that their horses had bolted from the noise was not accepted by the majority of the army!

The Benton Hussars (Joseph Nemitt's Cavalry Battalion) was raised in St Louis, Missouri, in late 1861, and wore a most distinctive costume, the usual colours being reversed in the light blue jacket and dark blue trousers. The black braiding on the jacket confirmed the 'Hussar' title, as did the 1851 pattern cloth shako, which latter item no doubt gave way to the képi once active service was commenced. Incorporating Von Deutsch's Milwaukee (Wisconsin) Cavalry Company (Company 'D', afterwards 'G') and Frémont's Bodyguard (Company 'G'), the Benton Hussars served with the Army of the West and the 1st Brigade, 2nd Division, Army of South-west Missouri until February 1862, when it was incorporated with the Hollan Horse into the 5th Missouri Cavalry, eventually passing into the 4th Missouri, which united both the Benton and Frémont Hussars.

11. U.S.A.: a) Officer, 1st
   Cavalry.
   b) Officer, 9th
   Vermont Cavalry.
   c) General of Cavalry.
The figures on this plate (all taken from contemporary photographs) show variations of the cavalry uniform as worn on campaign. The officer of the 1st U.S. Cavalry wears a civilian, fur-collared overcoat and civilian hat, with no visible badges of rank, only his pistol identifying him as a soldier.

The officer of the 9th Vermont Cavalry wears a type of 'patrol jacket', the other items of uniform being of the regulation pattern.

The General of Cavalry, taken from a photograph of Brigadier-General A. T. A. Torbert of Sheridan's staff, shows a uniform probably designed by the officer himself. The wearer's rank is indicated by the arrangement of the buttons and the rank-star worn on the collar and 'slouch' hat. This pattern of uniform was worn by other General officers: Custer wore a black velvet version with blue collar and Confederate-style cuff lacing, black breeches with gold stripe, with either a képi or black 'slouch' hat, the whole covered with yards of gold braid. While few officers approached this sartorial level, completely-regulation uniforms were few and far between in the later stages of the war.

12. U.S.A.: a) Officer, Infantry,
   Campaign Dress.
   b) Sergeant, 2nd
   Infantry, Full
   Dress.
   c) Officer, Infantry,
   Full Dress.
The regulation 'Hardee' hat, complete with plume, was worn in full dress by infantry officers, the badge on the front consisting of an embroidered hunting-horn badge (with

or without regimental identification). The frock-coat was double-breasted for field officers (i.e. from Major to Colonel), having two rows of buttons, seven in each, spaced equally. In full dress, epaulettes of a similar pattern to those of the cavalry were worn; otherwise, the same uniform was worn with embroidered rank-bars on the shoulders. Commissioned rank was further indicated by the universal red sash; either gloves or gauntlets were worn. Trousers (officially dark blue) were more often light blue with a ⅛th-inch wide seam-stripe.

On campaign, officers adopted numerous non-regulation variations; that illustrated is taken from a contemporary photograph. The képi bears a similar badge to that worn on the full-dress hat; the short jacket bears rank-bars and is worn with collar, tie and waistcoat. Officers' waistcoats were officially dark blue, white or buff with nine buttons and standing or 'rolled' collar, but numerous variations existed.

Other ranks wore a single-breasted frock-coat in full dress, piped with the infantry distinguishing colour (light blue), with brass shoulder-scales. The cords on the 'Hardee' hat were of the same colour as the piping. The badge of the hunting-horn with regimental and company identification was in brass for other ranks, borne on the front of the hat; when the hat was replaced with the képi for active service, these badges were transferred until discarded completely (as they frequently were). The 'Hardee' hat, though smart in appearance, was of little value in the field, and was replaced as soon as possible with the

képi, though not always officially; when the 111th Pennsylvania received their hats, they took the opportunity of ridding themselves of the unpopular headgear by throwing them into the river as the regimental train passed over the Shenandoah Bridge!

Sergeants wore the light-bladed N.C.O. sword in full dress, but not the sash, this being reserved for the ranks of 1st Sergeant and upwards. The Sergeants' trouser-stripe was 1½ inches wide.

13. U.S.A.: a) Corporal, Infantry, with National Flag.
b) Musician, Infantry, Full Dress.
c) Private, Infantry, Full Dress.

According to Regulations, each Federal regiment carried two colours, the National Flag (as illustrated) and the Regimental Flag. The National Flag, the 'Stars and Stripes', was six feet six inches long by six feet on the pole; the dark blue canton contained thirty-three white stars at the beginning of the war, later thirty-four when Kansas joined the Union (each star representing one state), and thirty-five from 1863 when West Virginia joined. The stars were arranged in a variety of designs, in rows, in a circle, in an oval, grouped around one large star, or arranged in the shape of one large star. Even the colour and design of individual stars varied, with five or occasionally seven points, sometimes of silver or gold. The regimental title was inscribed in the middle one (red) of the thirteen stripes, with battle-honours sometimes above and below. The fringe (where there was one) was yellow, and the tassels of mixed blue and white. The Regimental Flag was the same size as the National, of the same design as that of the Cavalry (Plate 6). Many corps, however – principally volunteer regiments – ignored the regulations completely, carrying the National Flag and the State Flag, or on occasion some independent pattern of their own invention.

The corporal illustrated (taken from a contemporary photograph) wears the regulation frock-coat without the shoulder-scales, and the black leather colour-belt. The képi bears the brass hunting-horn badge often discarded on active service.

This plate shows the full dress frock-coat, and the variation worn by musicians. The latter wore the standard infantry uniform with the addition of the distinctive lacing. common to all of the army, and on occasion a red worsted sash. However, in many cases this lacing was too distinctive, providing an excellent target for enemy sharpshooters, and as a result it was by no means uncommon for musicians to wear the simple, unmarked fatigue-coat like those of the rank and file. It was vital to shield musicians from enemy marksmen, as bugle and drum-calls were the only effective way of transmitting orders amid the noise of battle. Music also provided a great morale-boost: Lee declared that 'I don't believe we can have an army without music', while one drummer stated that when the band 'led the regiment . . . with their get-out-the-way-old-Dan-Tuckerish style of music, it made the men in the ranks step off as though they were bound for a Donnybrook Fair'. General Porter described how, at Five Forks in May 1865, one of Sheridan's mounted bands held their ground under heavy fire, 'Playing "Nelly Bly" as cheerfully as if it were furnishing music for a country picnic'.

The back view of the private illustrated shows the black leather cartridge-pouch with brass plate bearing the letters 'u.s.', and the black leather bayonet-scabbard with brass fittings.

14. U.S.A.: a) Private, 22nd New York Militia.
b) Private, Infantry, in greatcoat.
c) Company Officer, Infantry, Service Dress.

Although the 'Hardee' hat was the prescribed wear, many officers adopted the képi on active service. In the early stages of the war, the white linen cap-cover and neckcloth, named a 'Havelock' after the British general of the Indian Mutiny, was issued to many regiments, often two per man (one Connecticut unit received six per man!). Intended to be a protection against the heat of the sun, the 'Havelocks' were universally unpopular and were worn for only a short time: 'As it is made sufficiently large to cover the neck and shoulders, the effect, when properly adjusted, was to deprive the wearer of any air he might otherwise enjoy . . . prompted their immediate transfer to the plebeian uses of a dish-cloth or coffee-strainer ...'.

Officers of company rank (Lieutenants and Captains) wore single-breasted frock-coats (the double-breasted version being reserved for field officers); the frock was the common wear on active service, though more unusual varieties such as shell-jackets or fatigue-coats like those of the other ranks, with the addition of rank bars. The crimson sash was seldom worn on campaign; pistols were universal, many officers being armed with swords as well. The trousers had half-inch wide stripes.

The greatcoat worn by the rank and file was sky blue in colour, single-breasted with a cape reaching to the elbow with a 'stand-and-fall' collar. Equipment was worn over the great-coat but under the cape. Officers' overcoats were dark blue (see Plate 32) with four or more black silk loops across the breast. The coat had half-inch black silk edging and a knot on the sleeve denoting rank by its thickness: General – five braids, in double knot; Colonel – five, single knot; Lieutenant-Colonel – four; Major – three; Captain – two; 1st Lieutenant – one.

The first figure on this plate (taken from a contemporary photograph) shows the service uniform of the 22nd New York Militia (about 1862–63); of particular note is the 1855 pattern rifle with its long sword-bayonet.

15. U.S.A.: a) Drum Major, Infantry, Full Dress.
    b) Private, 42nd Pennsylvania Volunteers (Bucktails).
    c) 1st Sergeant, Infantry, Campaign Dress.

The uniforms of regimental bands were left to the discretion of the commanding officer of the regiment: he was allowed to 'make such additions in ornaments as he may judge proper.' Consequently, a bewildering variety of band uniforms were worn, some (like that illustrated) based upon the regulation uniform, but with the addition of plumed shakos or (in the case of drum-majors) huge bearskin caps. Other band uniforms were of gaudy colours (red or 'cadet grey' for example), with large amounts of coloured braid or metallic lace, sashes, gauntlets and every type of epaulette.

The other figures on this plate illustrate the typical uniform worn on campaign, based upon the regulation fatigue dress. The cloth képi ('shapeless as a feed bag') and often roomy enough to carry bits of clothing or other equipment on top of the head, officially bore the brass hunting horn badge and company distinguishing letter, but was more often than not discarded. The fatigue or 'sack' coat bore ordinary N.C.O. chevrons, and sergeants' rank was also indicated by the 1½-inch wide stripe on the trousers. Sergeant-Majors to 1st Sergeants were provided with red worsted sashes, but these were frequently omitted in campaign dress. The equipment shown is typical of that which might be worn before going into action, the knapsack with its restrictive straps being taken off. N.C.O.s were issued with a light-bladed sword which was rarely carried on campaign; it was suspended from a black leather shoulder-belt. To avoid the necessity of two shoulder-belts, sergeants carried the cartridge-pouch on the waist-belt. The black haversack and cloth-covered canteen (often with tin mug hanging from it) were like those carried by other ranks.

The Private of the 42nd Pennsylvania Volunteers shows the much more unorthodox version of campaign-equipment which became almost universal in both armies, with the cumbersome knapsack replaced by a rolled blanket containing the personal belongings and equipment. A unique distinction was the white 'bucktail' worn in the cap or hat, this custom supposedly arising from the fashion set by one James Landregan of Company 'I' who thought it would be an improvement to the drab képi with which he had been issued; the style so impressed Colonel Thomas Kane that he ordered all the regiment to follow suit, and announcing that his regiment would be known henceforth as 'The Bucktails'.

The regiments of Pennsylvania Volunteers numbered from 30th to 42nd inclusively were more commonly known as the 1st to 13th Pennsylvania Reserves. When the Government issued a call for volunteers, the state found a large excess of recruits to the authorised number, which Governor Andrew G. Curtin organised into the thirteen Reserve regiments, equipped and trained at state (rather than at Federal Govern-ment) expense. Organised in three brigades as the Pennsylvania Reserve Division, the corps served in the Peninsular Campaign, at Second Bull Run, Antietam and Fredericksburg, units then transferring from I Corps to the Army of the Potomac from Gettysburg to Spotsylvania. Mustering out in June 1864, a large number of men re-enlisted into the 190th and 191st Pennsylvania regiments, comprising the Veteran Reserve Brigade.

The 'Bucktails' (13th Reserves) was also known as the 1st Pennsylvania Rifles or the Kane Rifle Regiment, recruited principally from lumbermen who originally supplied their own rifles and who were generally excellent marksmen. The regiment was later armed with Sharps Rifles, and later still Spencers. Serving in the Peninsula, the Shenandoah Valley, Antietam, Fredericksburg, Gettysburg, the Wilderness and Spotsylvania, the regiment was also present in the last action fought by the Pennsylvania Reserves, Bethesda Church (1 June 1864), being mustered out ten days later, with a record of great distinction.

The various companies comprising the regiment were named as follows: 'A' Anderson Life Guards, 'B' Morgan Rifles, 'C' Cameron County Riflemen, 'D' Raftsmen's Guards or Warren Rifles, 'E' Tioga Rifles, 'F' Irish Infantry, 'G' Elk County Rifles, 'H' Wayne Independent Rifles, 'I' McKean County Rifles, 'K' Curwensville Rangers or Raftsmen's Rangers.

16. U.S.A.: a) Private, 20th Maine.

b) Corporal, Iron Brigade, First Uniform.

c) Private, Iron Brigade, Service Dress.

The private of the 20th Maine illustrated wears the ordinary fatigue uniform, but with the official regulation dark blue trousers; the regiment was one of the few to adhere to the original trousers rather than adopt the light blue ones authorised in December 1861. The figure shows the regulation infantry equipment, consisting of a waist-belt and small cap-pouch to the right of the brass plate, and a shoulder-belt supporting the cartridge-pouch on the right hip, the pouch having a tin liner and often a brass plate. On the left hip was worn a black waterproofed canvas haversack on a belt of the same material, and a tin water-canteen covered with buff, grey or blue worsted often with the letters 'U.S.' stencilled on, or left in the plain metal state. The black canvas haversack was often abandoned on campaign, its contents being carried rolled over one shoulder in the blanket, providing an extra protection against sword-cuts. A similar set of equipment was pre-scribed in Confederate regulations but the severe shortages and the in-dividual preference of the Confederate soldier resulted in much simpler equipment being almost universal in the Confederate army.

The Iron Brigade was perhaps the most famous unit to fight in the Civil War. Originally consisting of the 2nd, 6th and 7th Wisconsin and the 19th Indiana Regiments, the brigade was organised in October 1861 from small-town volunteers from the Western states, a small majority being native-born Americans, about 40 per cent Irish and Scandinavians, and a few English, Canadians and Germans. The brigade lost 33 per cent casualties at Second Bull Run, fighting five battles in three weeks and losing a total of 58 per cent of its original strength; joined by the 24th Michigan prior to the Antietam campaign, the formation gained its appropriate nickname of 'The Iron Brigade', coined by a war corres-pondent. After Fredericksburg and Chancellorsville, the Brigade en-tered the Gettysburg campaign as the 1st Brigade, 1st Division, I Corps. At Gettysburg the Brigade lost 1,200 men out of 1,800 engaged (the 24th Michigan 399 out of 496 – 80 per cent) which, on top of previous high casualties, destroyed the original Western Brigade; it was never as effective again when other troops were drafted in. But history records few formations to equal the consistent superb record of the Iron Brigade of the West.

The original uniforms of the Brigade were of the typical volunteer grey; the grey uniform of the 2nd Wisconsin caused considerable con-fusion at First Bull Run when the regiment was forced to retire in dis-order, having confused the Con-federate army with their own! The 6th Wisconsin mustered in civilian dress: 'a few wore broadcloth and silk hats, more the red shirts of raftsmen, several were in country homespun, one had a calico coat, and another was looking through a hole in the drooping brim of a straw hat'. They received a grey uniform similar to that of the 2nd, though many arrived in Washington with their 'uniform' consisting only of 'grey hats trimmed with green', one company being so undrilled that they were allowed to amble along at their own pace. In August 1861 the 19th Indiana arrived in Washington clad in 'grey doeskin cassimere and carrying Enfield or Minié rifles'.

By September 1861 all the grey costumes had been replaced by dark blue frock-coats, 'Hardee' hats, light blue trousers and white gaiters; thus originated their nickname of 'The Black Hat Brigade'. This was the classic uniform of the Brigade, though the ravages of campaigning soon took their toll: by 1863 the frock-coat had been replaced by the fatigue-coat in perhaps half the brigade, though photographs show the two being worn even within the same company. The unpopular gaiters were soon thrown away, as were the hat-ornaments, this item becoming progressively more battered and shapeless. Some officers preferred the képi, but most of the Brigade clung to the 'Hardee' hat as a jealously-guarded unique distinguishing feature. The 24th Michigan, the last to join the brigade, wore the ordinary fatigue-coat and képi.

The Iron Brigade of the West should not be confused with John Porter Hatch's Iron Brigade, consisting of the 2nd, 24th, 30th and 84th New York and the 2nd U.S. Sharpshooters, which was broken up in May 1863.

17. U.S.A.: a) Private, 21st Michigan, Service Dress.
b) Private, Irish Brigade.
c) Private, 8th Wisconsin, Service Dress.

The figures of the 21st Michigan and 8th Wisconsin (both taken from contemporary photographs) show typical variations of the campaign uniform. The 21st Michigan almost entirely wore battered black 'slouch' hats with or without leather bands; the fatigue-blouse in this case worn with the top button unfastened and the lapels turned back, though a number of full dress frock-coats were also worn.

The 8th Wisconsin apparently largely retained the frock-coat with the ubiquitous battered hat. The regiment was known as 'The Eagle Regiment' from their custom of taking the regimental mascot – an eagle – into battle with them, sitting on a specially-constructed perch. The eagle, named 'Old Abe' after President Lincoln, achieved fame by becoming the subject of a popular song ('Old Abe the Battle Eagle') by J. Bates and T. Martin Towne. After the war, the eagle passed into honourable retirement, maintained at state expense in Milwaukee. The companies of the 8th retained the titles of the small companies from which the regiment had been formed: Company 'A' Wanapaca Union Rifles, 'B' Sheboygan County Independents, 'C' Eau Claire Eagles, 'D' Fox Lake Volunteer Rifles, 'E' Rough and Ready Guards, 'F' Crawford County Volunteers, 'G'

Janesville Fire Zouaves, 'H' Sugar River Rifles, 'I' La Crosse County Rifles, 'K' Racine County Volunteers.

The Irish Brigade (1st Division, II Corps, Army of the Potomac) was originally composed of the 63rd, 69th and 88th New York, being the 3rd, 1st and 4th/5th Regiments of Thomas Francis Meagher's Irish Brigade respectively, being raised from Irish immigrants in New York by Meagher, who had been transported from Ireland to Tasmania in 1852 for treason and sedition. In autumn 1862 the 28th Massachusetts (2nd Irish Regiment) and the 166th Pennsylvania were added, the latter being transferred out in July 1864. The 29th Massachusetts (2nd Regiment, Meagher's Brigade) served from June to November 1862, the 7th New York Heavy Artillery being added in September 1864. The Brigade especially distinguished itself at Fredericksburg and Antietam.

The Irish Brigade wore a distinctive uniform, consisting of the regulation fatigue coat with the addition of green collars and cuffs, and grey trousers; the badge worn on top of the képi was a red clover-leaf. To emphasise their Irish origin, each regiment carried a green flag in addition to their regulation colours.

The 28th Massachusetts was also known as the Faugh-a-Ballagh Regiment, this name being a Gaelic war-cry meaning 'clear the way'.

18. **U.S.A.: a) Officer, 5th New York Zouaves, Full Dress.**
b) Zouave, Campaign

Dress.
c) Private, 5th New York Zouaves, Full Dress.

Mustered into service on 9 May 1861 for a two-year enlistment, the 5th New York (Duryée Zouaves) was one of the best units to serve in the Union army. Justly famous under its first commander, Abram Duryée (a New York merchant long active in the State Militia) for its precise parade-ground drill, the 5th won the admiration of the regular regiment of Sykes' Division in V Corps in which it spent all its service, when at Gaines' Mill, under a heavy fire, the regiment coolly paused to 'count off' and realign its ranks after having sustained heavy casualties. Under Duryée and the Colonels who succeeded him (Gouverneur Kemble Warren and Hiram Duryea) the 5th maintained a magnificent record in action; when the regiment's enlistment expired on 14 May 1863, a large number of three-year enlistees transferred to the 146th New York. Another regiment bearing the same number was raised by Colonel Cleveland Winslow which rejoined V Corps to serve out the war. The 5th New York also bore the name 'National Zouaves'; it should not be confused with the 2nd Duryée Zouaves (165th New York).

The Zouaves fashion sprang into favour before the outbreak of the war, when drill-teams dressed to resemble the élite French light infantry gave public displays throughout the country. Volunteer and militia companies copied the style extensively. The 5th New York wore a typical Zouave costume: fez with white turban wound round for parade, the blue-tasselled cap being worn alone on service. The rank and file wore the conventional Zouave jacket and shirt, with 'baggy' trousers tucked into high gaiters. In common with most Zouave units, officers wore a modified version of the regulation uniform, basically, the frock-coat with Confederate-style cuff-braid, red képi and trousers.

Despite their reputation, British war correspondent William Howard Russell (who had seen the genuine French Zouaves) was unimpressed by the 5th New York; some men wore the turban without the fez underneath, so that their hair stuck through the 'discoloured napkins', while Russell considered the trousers – 'loose bags of red calico' – to be quite 'ridiculous'; the net effect being 'a line of military scarecrows'. A less critical eye, however, would have been most impressed with the regiment's colour-guard, many of whom were approaching seven feet in height.

The Zoauve officer in campaign dress (taken from a contemporary photograph) shows how the uniform was modified on campaign; only the stocking-cap identifies the man as a member of a Zouave unit.

Volunteers (Hawkins' Zouaves) was recruited. Enlistees included men from Albany, Brooklyn, Hyde Park, Mt Vernon, Staten Island, Connecticut, New Jersey and Canada. It was engaged in the Maryland Campaign, South Mountain, Antietam and in Eastern Virginia. The 9th was mustered out on 20 May 1863, having lost 358 officers and men on active service.

Uniform for the rank and file was of the typical Zouave style, of blue with magenta or purple trimming; sashes were light blue or purple, and greatcoats were light blue. Rank chevrons were of the regimental facing colour. In full dress officers also wore a Zouave-style uniform with shako, but it is likely that on campaign a more regulation style would be adopted.

Rush Hawkins was discharged as Brevet-Brigadier-General on the same day as the 9th were mustered out; having made a fortune from real estate and investments, he became famous for the collection of fifteenth-century books and printed material formed by his wife and himself, a collection rivalled only by that of the British Museum.

19. U.S.A.: a) Private, 9th New York Volunteers.
b) Officer, 9th New York Volunteers.

Serving in the U.S.–Mexican war whilst still a teenager, Rush Christopher Hawkins was originally president of a military club formed in 1860 from which the 9th New York

20. U.S.A.: 79th New York Volunteers, 1861.
a) Private, Full Dress.
b) Private, Service Dress.
c) Sergeant, Full Dress.

Formed at the suggestion of Captain Roderick of the British Consulate on 9 October 1859, this regiment of New

York State Militia took its name and number from the 79th (Cameron) Highlanders of the British army, its four companies being composed of Scottish immigrants. Called into Federal service on 18 May 1861, the regiment's strength was increased to 1,000 by the recruitment of Scottish, Irish and English New Yorkers, with a few of other nationalities. The Pipe and Drum band being seconded for duty at the White House, the regiment fought at First Bull Run where the commander, Colonel James Cameron, was killed. The 79th had always elected its own officers, but when Isaac Ingalls Stevens was appointed in Cameron's stead without the regiment's approval, there occurred a minor 'mutiny' as a protest. Stevens was reluctantly accepted when the regimental colours were confiscated as a punishment for the 'mutiny', but were returned after Second Bull Run as a reward for the 79th's valiant conduct. Stevens, who became extremely popular with the regiment, was killed at Chantilly with the colours in his hands, having taken them from the sixth colour-bearer to have fallen. After serving with distinction in fifty-nine engagements, the 79th was mustered out on 13 May 1863, the men with unexpired terms forming two companies of the New Cameron Highlanders. The regiment was disbanded as a regiment of New York State Militia in January 1876.

As befitted a regiment of Scottish origins, the 79th wore a most distinctive costume. In full dress a Scottish doublet was worn, with red shoulder-straps bearing the numerals '79' in brass, red cuff-patches piped light blue, with collar of either red edged light blue, or light blue with red and white patch. The rear tails of the doublet bore embroidered yellow grenades. With this uniform was worn a Glengarry cap in full dress, with diced border and brass badge; there was a regimental badge prior to the war but this was later replaced by a replica of the State seal. Kilts and truibhs (trews) were worn in full dress, of Cameron of Erracht tartan like those of their counterparts in the British army. With the kilt was worn a white hair sporran with black 'tails' and a white metal thistle badge, diced hose, red garters and black shoes with silver buckles. N.C.O.s wore red sashes and yellow epaulettes; chevrons were light blue and their swords were of a typically-Scottish pattern.

The regulation képi was also worn, having a brass badge in the form of a hunting horn with '79' in the centre; the equipment was of the standard U.S. issue. The Scottish costume soon disappeared when active campaigning began, like the more exotic costume of other volunteer regiments; even before First Bull Run many had abandoned the kilt and truibhs for the regulation light blue trousers as illustrated. However, some of the former were worn at the battle, as confirmed by photographs of prisoners wearing kilts and truibhs; and one unnamed Captain is recorded as having been loudly cheered for chasing a chicken over a fence whilst wearing a kilt! Those kilts worn on active service were probably protected by buff aprons bearing '79' in large white numerals on the front.

By the end of the war, however, all

traces of Scotitsh costume had disappeared; the Ladies of the Scottish Society of New York sent new glengarries to the regiment to wear on their re-entry into the city after mustering out on 14 June 1865.

21. U.S.A.: a) Private, 39th New York Volunteers (Garibaldi Guard).
    b) Private, 1st Massachusetts Militia.
    c) Corporal, Vermont Brigade.

Many of the New York regiments were organised on a 'national' basis, companies being composed of men of the same national origin – for example, part of the 36th New York was known as The British Volunteers. Most famous was the 39th New York, known as The Garibaldi Guard or the 1st Foreign Rifles.

Mustered on 28 May 1861, the regiment included one company of Italians, one of French, 3 German, 3 Hungarian, one Spanish and one Swiss, named after the famous Italian patriot and uniformed in a Franco-Italian style including the distinctive Italian 'Bersaglieri' hat with plume of cocks' feathers and the brass letters 'G.G.' on the front. The uniform was of an Italian style; the red roll was frequently worn over the shoulder. Officers had the same uniform, with the addition of normal rank-markings and fringed epaulettes.

The Garibaldi Guard even included Cantinière girls of the French style, these ladies being equipped with barrels of water and spirits intended to give aid to wounded soldiers. Their costume was copied from their French counterparts – small black Bersaglieri hat with green plume; red waist-length jacket worn open to expose a white blouse and black 'string' tie, single-breasted with white shoulder-straps, red turned-back lapels, red collar and pointed cuffs, all edged with gold lace; black girdle with red edges; voluminous blue skirt, several inches above the knee, edged with red lace; dark blue trousers with red stripe down the outer seams worn under the skirt; and a small wooden barrel worn over the right shoulder on a black leather belt. The regiment carried three colours, having an unofficial standard based upon the Italian tricolour of red, white, and green in addition to the National and Regimental colours.

Two months after muster, the 39th served at First Bull Run, but was captured at Harper's Ferry on 15 September 1862. It served out its four-year enlistment after a prisoner-exchange, being engaged at Gettysburg. It should not be confused with the Garibaldi Legion (Louisiana volunteers) or the Garibaldi Guard (Company 'B', 9th Pennsylvania Reserves).

The uniform of the 1st Massachusetts Militia illustrated is almost identical to the fatigue uniform of the regular army during the U.S.–Mexican War (1846–48), consisting of light blue/grey shell-jacket and trousers, the only difference being the head-dress, the regulation képi replacing the earlier forage cap. As in the Mexican War, officers wore the regulation dark blue frock-coat in place of the shell-jacket. The 1st Massachusetts Militia became part of the 1st Massachusetts Infantry, though Company 'C' (Massachusetts True Blues) became Company 'K' of the 6th Militia.

The Vermont Brigade, consisting of the 2nd, 3rd, 4th, 5th and 6th ermont Regiments, was clothed ompletely in grey in the early part of the war, with regiments distinguished by the colour of their facings and trouser-stripes, the 2nd having green, the 3rd red, the 4th dark blue, the 5th black and the 6th light blue. This brigade, justly among the most famous of the war, suffered the highest casualties of any Federal brigade: in a week's fighting at the Wilderness and Spotsylvania, for example, it lost 1,645 men out of a total of 2,800. The uniform illustrated (taken from a contemporary photograph) shows the uniform adopted to replace the original grey; it is interesting to note that the corporal wears small gauntlets; in the photograph mentioned, only one soldier (on whom the illustration is based) wears these non-regulation items.

22. U.S.A.: a) Private, 7th New York National Guard.
    b) Corporal, 7th New York National Guard.
    c) Sergeant, New York Militia.

Tracing their descent to 1806, the title of the 7th New York National Guard was adopted by the regiment in 1847. An active force in city riot-control, the more unruly members of the mob christened the 7th 'the old greybacks', their dislike of the part-time soldiers being increased by the fact that all ranks were drawn from the highest-ranked members of the community, enlistment in the 7th being considered more like an exclusive club. Under the command of Abram Duryée (later of Zouave fame) from 1849 to 1859 the regiment became the most famous 'civilian' corps in the country. Members served a seven-year enlistment, purchased their own uniform and drilled once a week for ten months of the year, benefiting in return for their service by exemption from jury duty and a deduction on city property tax.

When Washington was briefly menaced at the outbreak of the war, President Lincoln appealed for state militia to come to the aid of the few regulars awaiting the expected Confederate attack on the capital. The 7th New York volunteered to a man, and were given a rapturous send-off in a parade down Broadway when they left, 1,000 strong, on 19 April under Colonel Marshall Lefferts. Travelling to Philadelphia by train (where they were issued with twenty-four rounds of ammunition per man when news came of an attack on the 6th Massachusetts Militia by a rebel mob in Baltimore), they found rail communications severed by saboteurs. Lefferts therefore chartered a steamship at his own expense to Annapolis, completing the journey by train to Washington, the whole corps reporting personally to the White House. Followed by other volunteer corps, the threat to Washington was averted. The 7th New York returned home after serving a term of garrison duty in Washington, reverting to militia status, though its members were eagerly sought to become officers in other volunteer units forming for the war; over 600 served with distinction in the Federal army.

The uniform of the 7th was of the typical pre-war militia style, consisting of képi, shell-jacket and trousers of light grey with black trimming. The képi bore the company number on the front in a small brass numeral. The brass waist-belt plate bore the initials 'N.G.' and the company number (in letters); the cypher 'N.G.' was repeated in ornate lettering in the cartridge-pouch. Equipment consisted of canteen, knapsack, buff or black oilskin haversack, leather-covered mess-pail strapped to the rear of the knapsack, and a red blanket. White leather equipment was worn from 1849 until 1861. In 1853 shakos were issued, but these were reserved for full dress. Greatcoats were light blue; the regiment was armed with the 1855 Rifle musket.

The third figure on this plate (taken from a contemporary painting) shows the influence of French styles in the uniform of another New York Militia corps.

23. U.S.A.: a) Officer, 1st Rhode Island Volunteers.
b) Private, 1st Rhode Island Volunteers.
c) Private, 2nd New Hampshire Volunteers.

The 1st Rhode Island Volunteers was organised around Providence, and commanded by Ambrose Everett Burnside, later to become General. The 1st Rhode Island engaged for a three-month enlistment beginning 20 April 1861 and ending on 2 August of the same year. It served at First Bull Run, where, though performing well in the early stages of the action, became entangled in the general rout which followed.

The uniform was remarkably different from other Union volunteer corps, both 1st and 2nd Rhode Island wearing at least two and possibly three distinct styles of blouse, known as 'Burnside' or 'Rhode Island' blouses. One, of plain blue cloth, very nearly resembled the classic 'hunting shirt' beloved of American 'backwoodsmen' for generations; another similar blouse had a pleated front and very wide collar was referred to as a 'hunting jacket'; the third was of the same length but with a buttoned-on 'plastron' front and standing collar, probably inspired by the dress of the numerous volunteer fire-fighting companies from which many volunteer regiments were raised. Trousers were either grey or light blue; the red blanket, normally worn rolled across the body, could be worn as a 'poncho' by means of a slit cut in the middle to act as a neck-hole.

The 1st Rhode Island had a Vivandière (sutleress), one Kady Brownell, daughter of a British soldier, born on campaign in Africa. She followed her husband, Robert S. Brownell, into the 1st Rhode Island, though forsook her appointment to fight alongside the men with rifle and sword. Transferring into the 5th

Rhode Island at the end of the three months' enlistment, Kady left the army when Robert was invalided out after being wounded at New Bern, when she returned to being a housewife, complete with discharge certificate signed by Burnside and her sword! The officer illustrated is carrying a Beaumont-Adams revolver.

The 2nd New Hampshire Volunteers served in Burnside's Brigade at First Bull Run, where the regiment, though involved in the rout, was able to withdraw from the flight and reform in good order. Thereafter it served in every major engagement fought by the Army of the Potomac until mustered out on 19 December 1865. The regiment wore one of the most archaic uniforms of the war in the early months of its service, consisting of a long tailcoat with red turnbacks, lining, and piping, the whole being of volunteer grey. Leather equipment was apparently either white or black. Officers probably wore a similar style of dress, or perhaps the more regulation dark blue frock-coat.

24. U.S.A.: a) Sergeant with marker flag, 14th New York Volunteers.
b) Sergeant, Company 'D', 19th Illinois Volunteers (Ellsworth Zouave Cadets).

Ephraim Elmer Ellsworth (after whom Company 'D' of the 19th Illinois was named as Ellsworth's Zouave Cadets) could be considered the instigator of the 'Zouave movement' in America. Before the war he was famous for the spectacular drill displays given by his Chicago Zouaves (Companies 'A' and 'K' of the 19th Illinois when the war commenced) in tours throughout the country, which without doubt was the main reason for the popularity of the Zouave style among militia companies of both North and South, all wishing to emulate Ellsworth's gaudy unit. In August 1860 the Chicago Zouaves gave a display on the White House lawn; when war threatened, Ellsworth raised the 11th New York Volunteers, known as Ellsworth's Zouaves or the 1st New York Fire Zouaves, the latter name coming from its composition, the recruits being drawn mainly from volunteer fire-fighting companies. On 24 May 1861 Ellsworth was removing a Confederate flag from the roof of the Marshall House Tavern in Alexandria when he was shot and killed by the proprietor, a Southern sympathiser named James T. Jackson. Jackson himself was immediately killed by Private Francis Edwin Brownell of 'A' Company of the 11th New York, for which he was awarded the Congressional Medal of Honour. Insignificant though the incident was, it was witnessed by a correspondent of the New York *Tribune*, whose report caused a sensation and turned Ellsworth into a national hero overnight, doing much to arouse war sentiments in the North as well as to popularise the Zouave-style of unit even further.

The 14th New York Militia (later 84th New York Infantry [The

Brooklyn Chasseurs]) were uniformed to resemble the Chasseurs à Pied (light infantry) of the French army, though contemporary reports of 'red-legged zouaves' of the 14th at Antietam confused the two French styles. The képi of the 14th bore the numerals '14' on the front, and was further distinguished by the blue circle on the crown. Though the jacket appeared to have been worn over a red shirt, the jacket and 'shirt' were in fact one garment, the blue sewn onto the red, the buttons on the blue being purely decorative. The detachable 'trefoil' epaulettes were worn by all ranks; the canvas gaiters buttoned up the side. The cap-pouch on the waistbelt was ornamented with a brass State device consisting of an eagle with outstretched wings over a shield, over a scroll; the waist-belt plate bore the State device of 's.n.y.' ('State of New York', interpreted by the Confederates as 'Snotty-Nosed Yanks'!) Officers wore a more regulation uniform or frock-coat, but with the regimental red trousers which had a gold lace stripe down the outer seam.

The sergeant illustrated is carrying a marker flag attached to the muzzle of his rifle; these small standards were used to enable the men to keep their 'dressing' in action; based upon the National flag, the blue canton contained the regimental number surrounded by thirteen stars, indicative of the original thirteen colonies forming the United States.

The 14th New York (and the 84th which it became) included an engineer company, Butt's Company of Sappers and Miners. Though not as fashionable as Zouave units, there were a considerable number of Chasseur corps in both armies – for example, the 7th Battalion Louisiana Infantry of the Confederacy were known as Chasseurs à Pied or the St Paul's Foot Rifles, the latter being an unusual 'anglicization' of the original French name.

25. U.S.A.: a) Private, 4th Michigan Volunteers.
b) Private, 4th Michigan Volunteers.
c) Officer, 11th Indiana Volunteers.

The 4th Michigan Volunteers were organised at Adrian on 16 May 1861, and served throughout the war with a distinguished record, winning particular distinction in the five days of action at Gaines' Mill and Malvern Hill (where the regiment sustained 252 casualties), and at a desperate hand-to-hand fight in 'The Wheat Field' at Gettysburg, where the 4th lost 165 men and Colonel Harrison Jeffords, killed defending the regimental colours. The 4th Michigan were distinguished by the Zouave-style stocking-cap with red tassel, worn with the regulation uniform, though apparently the képi was also extensively worn. The dark blue trousers and tan gaiters were another regimental distinction. Officers probably wore regulation infantry uniform. Company designations were as follows: Company 'A' Smith Guard; 'B' Adrian Volunteers; 'C' Peninsular

Guard; 'D' Barry Guard; 'E' Hillsdale Volunteers; 'F' Hudson Volunteers; 'G' Tecumseh Volunteers; 'H' Grosvenor Guard; 'I' Trenton Volunteers; 'K' Dexter Union Guard.

Zouave regiments were not popular in the Western states; the frontiersmen realised the foolishness of making themselves such excellent targets by wearing gaudy uniforms. The 11th Indiana Volunteers were a notable exception, though their uniform was sensibly plain, of 'the tamest gray twilled goods not unlike home-made jeans', 'Greekish in form', with trousers 'baggy but not petticoated'. The grey uniforms, instead of making the regiment an unduly good target, made them in line appear like 'a smoky ribbon long drawn out'. The rank and file wore a similar uniform to that illustrated, with tan or white gaiters and light grey overcoats.

The 11th Indiana was formed from independent companies, enlisting in April 1861 for a three-month term of service, twice re-enlisting for a three-year and later an eighteen-month term of service, ending 26 July 1865. The regiment's distinguished record included service at Shiloh, Antietam, Gettysburg, Chickamauga and the Wilderness. Named 'The Wallace Zouaves' after their Colonel, Lewis Wallace, the regiment's fame is somewhat eclipsed by that of its leader. Lew Wallace rose to Major-General, served on the court-martial board of Lincoln's assassins, was president of the court-martial which convicted Henry Wirz, commander of the infamous Andersonville prison camp, and was appointed U.S. Minister to Turkey (1881–85). He is best remembered as Governor of New Mexico, in which office he was instrumental in the demise of William H. Bonney, the murderer and desperado known as Billy the Kid, and for being the author of *Ben Hur*.

26. U.S.A.: a) Private, 83rd Pennsylvania Volunteers.
b) Drummer, 114th Pennsylvania Volunteers.
c) Private, 114th Pennsylvania Volunteers.

C. H. T. Collis, an Irish-born captain, organised an independent company of Pennsylvania Zouaves to act as bodyguard to General N. P. Banks, the company containing a large number of Frenchmen who had served as Zouaves in the French army. Banks' Bodyguard, or the Zouaves d'Afrique, so impressed General Banks that Charles Collis was sent back to Philadelphia to recruit a full regiment, based upon his original company, which became Company 'A' of the new regiment, the 114th Pennsylvania Volunteers (Collis' Zouaves). This regiment wore the same uniform as the earlier Independent Company, materials being specially imported from France. Unlike many Zouave units, the 114th maintained their distinctive uniform throughout their service, with little modification for the hardships of campaign; on occasion, the gaiters appear to have been discarded, though a photograph of Company 'F' taken near Petersburg in August 1864 shows the complete uniform in use. Officers wore the regulation uniform but with red trousers; the regimental band appear to have worn Zouave costume with képis instead of the usual fez and turban. The earlier title of 'Zouaves d'Afrique' was maintained by the 114th, the oval plates of their cartridge-pouches bearing the embossed lettering '114 REGT. Z.D'A. P.V.'

The 83rd Pennsylvania (The Erie Regiment), 'one of the very best regiments in the army' according to General McClellan, wore imported French uniforms described as being the 'Chasseurs de Vincennes' pattern; basically, this was the regulation French light infantry uniform. Unfortunately, these uniforms being made for Frenchmen, most were too small for the large Pennsylvanians of the 83rd, giving a slightly ridiculous appearance of short sleeves and trousers! Each man was issued with a shako, dress and fatigue uniforms, cloak, two pairs of shoes, two pairs of white gloves, two nightcaps and gaiters. When the regiment left for the Peninsula in the spring of 1862, the French uniforms were put into store and ordinary fatigue-dress issued in their stead.

27. U.S.A.: 1st Sharpshooters.
a) Officer.
b) Corporal.

Riflemen always having been a legendary American arm of service, the idea of forming two regiments of outstanding marksmen was conceived by Hiram Berdan, himself a champion rifle-shot for fifteen years prior to the war, who, though considered 'thoroughly unscrupulous and unreliable' by some was an outstanding inventor whose various gadgets included a repeating rifle, a 'submarine gunboat' and a distance-fuze for shrapnel.

Organising his two regiments, Berdan was appointed Colonel of the 1st U.S. Sharpshooters, with Colonel H. A. Post to command the 2nd. All recruits were required to place ten consecutive shots within five inches of a bullseye at 200 yards to be accepted, and originally provided their own rifles; this latter practice naturally caused difficulties of ammunition-supply, so Berdan requested an issue of Sharps rifles. They received only muzzle-loading Springfields, until a remarkable display of marksmanship by Berdan himself brought Lincoln's personal intervention, resulting in the issue of the desired Sharps rifles. Almost invariably both regiments were deployed in small groups of snipers and skirmishers, in which duty they excelled Berdan's wildest hopes; it has been calculated that they killed more Confederates than any other regiment in the army. Many of their exploits are legendary; in the Peninsular Campaign, for example, a small party of Sharpshooters silenced a Confederate battery for an hour by shooting the gunners at the range of half a mile! The 1st Regiment fought at Chancellorsville (where its skirmishers captured the 23rd Georgia) and at Gettysburg; the 2nd served at Antietam, and thereafter mostly alongside the 1st Regiment.

The uniform of the two Sharpshooter regiments was as unusual as their rôle. The dark green képi was decorated with badges of brass crossed rifles with the letters 's.s.' and 'u.s.' worn on occasion by the rank and file, whilst officers wore the letters 'u.s.s.s.' surrounded by a wreath in gold embroidery on the crown of the cap. Corps badges were later worn on the képi: a red diamond for example when the Sharpshooters formed part of the 1st Division, III Corps. In full dress a black feather plume was worn on the cap, and often black, brown or grey 'slouch' hats on campaign. The dark green frock-coats were worn by all ranks, N.C.O.s' chevrons being either light blue or dark green on a light blue patch. Trousers were originally light blue, but were later changed to green to match the rest of the uniform and were often worn with long black or brown leather gaiters. Officers wore crimson sashes; equipment was of black leather, though knapsacks were made of goatskin with the hair left on. Cartridge-pouches bore oval brass plates with the letters 'u.s.' embossed (the same design as the belt-plates) and were carried by all ranks, officers being armed with rifles in addition to the usual pistol. Great-coats were either grey (sometimes trimmed with dark green) or light blue; equipment was usually discarded in action to allow maximum freedom of movement. Non-reflective rubber buttons were used at one time.

In addition to the Sharps rifle, a number of .56 Colt revolving rifles were used, these being most unpopular due to the tendency of blowing up in the face of the owner! Some selected marksmen carried heavy, precision-made snipers' rifles with telescopic sights for even greater accuracy.

The 1st Regiment had ten companies, the second eight, each company being drawn from one state and bearing the state's name. In the 1st Regiment, the companies were as follows: Company 'A' New York, 'B' New York, 'C' Michigan, 'D' New York, 'E' 1st New Hampshire, 'F' 1st Vermont, 'G' Wisconsin, 'H' New York, 'I' Michigan, 'K' Michigan; an eleventh company, 'L', existed for a time, being designated as the 2nd Minnesota, being later transferred to the 1st Minnesota Infantry. In the 2nd Regiment, company designations were: 'A' 1st Minnesota, 'B' Michigan, 'C' Independent Pennsylvania Sharpshooters, 'D' 1st Maine, 'E' 2nd Vermont, 'F' 2nd New Hampshire, 'G' 3rd New Hampshire, and 'H' 3rd Vermont.

28. U.S.A.: a) Sergeant, 1st Heavy Artillery, Corps d'Afrique.
    b) 1st Sergeant, 56th U.S. Coloured Infantry.
    c) Private, U.S. Coloured Infantry.

Beginning with the Corps d'Afrique (Louisiana Native Guards) and the 1st Louisiana National Guard, the first 'black' regiment in U.S. service (mustered 27 September 1862), about 300,000 coloured troops were enrolled in Federal service following the Emancipation Proclamation (1 January 1863) in 166 regiments (145 infantry, seven cavalry, twelve heavy artillery, one field artillery, one engineer), of which about sixty were employed in the field. Officers were white; negro regiments, though they behaved admirably in action, were not extensively used in battle: 143 officers and 2,751 men were killed in action. XXV Corps was reorganised late in the war to consist entirely of negro corps, use of such troops being restricted almost entirely to the Union. Racial feelings were such in the Confederacy that (though a regiment of negroes was raised in New Orleans in 1863) the use of coloured troops was not seriously considered until the war was almost over, when 300,000 slaves were conscripted in March 1865; though a few companies were formed, none were used.

The 1st Heavy Artillery of the Corps d'Afrique (previously the 1st Louisiana Heavy Artillery (African Descent)), formed part of the garrison of New Orleans, manning some of the batteries which protected the stronghold. Their uniform was basically the artillery full dress, with the battery identification letter borne above the crossed cannons badge on the hat. The New Orleans sector being comparatively quiet, the troops there were able to maintain their uniforms near to the full dress regulations, never having to succumb to the more ragged appearance of their more heavily-engaged comrades in other theatres of war. The sidearm was the 1833 pattern Foot Artillery sword, a copy of the French weapon originally based on the ancient Roman gladius.

Other coloured regiments wore standard fatigue uniform with no special distinctions, except that in many cases many regiments received uniforms of excellent quality, the normal coarse cloth having temporarily run out at the time the coloured regiments were raised. This plate, however, illustrates two variations, both taken from contemporary photographs. The private wears the regulation full-dress frock-coat with the collar turned down, and has a képi covered in a black 'waterproof', a common addition in wet weather. The 1st Sergeant of the 56th Coloured Infantry (originally the 3rd Arkansas Infantry [African Descent]) wears what appears to be a shell-jacket, but which was, in fact, a cut-down frock-coat (note the piping on collar and cuffs).

Exactly what uniform the Confederate slave regiments were intended to wear is doubtful, but the Charleston *Evening News* of 1 May 1861 noted a company of '125 free Negroes' uniformed in 'red shirts and dark pants' and bearing the Confederate flag; these were almost certainly an engineer or civilian labour unit.

29. U.S.A.: a) Drummer, 1st Artillery.
b) Private, 1st Artillery.

This plate shows the Artillery full dress uniform, basically the standard infantry style with red piping and hat-cords, the distinctive colour of the artillery arm of service. Hat-badges consisted of crossed cannon-barrels with regimental and company distinctives; equipment was on infantry pattern, with the unserviceable 1833 pattern artillery sword. This uniform, like that of the infantry, was almost immediately replaced on active service by the képi and fatigue-blouse, though occasionally items of the full dress were retained for a time: for example, a photograph of a mortar battery at Yorktown in 1862 shows a sentry dressed in fatigue uniform and full equipment, yet still wearing the brass shoulder-scales. The drummer wears the usual braiding on the breast in the red distinctive colour.

The Federal Government issued 7,892 fieldpieces to the five Regular artillery regiments, and to the fifty-seven regiments, seventeen battalions and 380 independent companies of Volunteer artillery.

30. U.S.A.: a) 1st Lieutenant, 2nd Artillery, Service Dress, 1862.
   b) 1st Lieutenant, 14th Ohio Volunteer Light Artillery, 1864.
   c) Gunner, Light Artillery, Full Dress.

The U.S. Artillery was divided into two branches, Artillery and Light Artillery, the latter roughly approximating to the 'horse artillery' (i.e. the more mobile) of European armies. There was no clearly-defined distinction between the two, both operating 'medium' fieldpieces, the heavier siege-guns and mortars being the responsibility of the heavy arm. The lack of precise distinction between the two arms is shown by the fact that some ordinary artillery regiments included totally mounted batteries: Battery 'B' of the 4th Artillery, for example, served as Light [horse] Artillery in the Indian and Mormon campaigns of the 1850's.

In uniform, however, there was a much clearer distinction, the light artillery having a style of dress corresponding to that of their European counterparts. The blue cloth shako with hanging plume and red cords bore a brass crossed-cannons badge on the front, together with a U.S. shield badge. Apparently there were two styles of shako-badge in use, those of about 1861–62 having ornaments of the 1830's pattern, while those of the later period used badges normally worn on the 'Hardee' hat. The remainder of the uniform, consisting of shell-jacket and trousers (cut loose to spread over the boot) was in obvious cavalry style, whilst maintaining the red distinctive colour in the form of piping. The light artillery was the one arm never ordered to wear the dark blue trousers which were replaced in the rest of the army by the more familiar light blue. The full-dress uniform was almost immediately replaced by the standard fatigue dress when active service commenced: indeed, it is doubtful whether many volunteer light artillery units ever received the shakos and shell-jackets. The sabre carried was the 1840 pattern light artillery weapon, with very long black leather knot; when available, pistols were also carried by all ranks.

As with other branches of the army, the service uniform for officers of artillery consisted of frock-coat with rank bars, light blue trousers with red stripe, either képi or felt hat, and crimson silk sash. The uniform of the 14th Ohio Light Artillery illustrated (taken from a photograph of 1st Lieutenant Thomas Jeffery) shows a variation on this uniform; the hat-badge consisted of a simple design of crossed cannon-barrels instead of the prescribed gold-embroidered cannon with silver regimental number beneath, on a backing of black velvet; the sash was omitted, and a black leather telescope-case was hung from one shoulder.

The other figure (taken from photographs of Lieutenant-Colonel William Hays and 1st Lieutenant William N. Dennison of the 2nd Artillery) wears a more unorthodox and yet very common style of uniform, consisting of an other ranks' fatigue blouse with rank-bars sewn on, with shirt and scarf underneath. The hat, with small brim, was of a not unusual style; another officer in the aforementioned photograph wears a crossed cannon-barrels badge high up on the front of such a hat. Not all officers carried sabres, but the pistol was an almost universal sidearm. Buff or light brown gauntlets were common to officers of all branches of both armies. Light artillery officers for 'undress duty' were allowed to wear short blue jackets with red trimming, similar to that worn by the rank and file, with the addition of appropriate rank insignia.

31. U.S.A.: a) U.S. Ordnance Sergeant, Full

Dress.
b) 1st Sergeant,
U.S. Engineers,
Full Dress.
The Ordnance Corps was responsible for the issue and maintenance of weapons in the field, for armouries and for gun-foundries operated at government arsenals, duties vital to the maintenance of an army. In 1861 two corps of Engineers existed, one of Topographical Engineers, with a total strength of 105 officers and 750 other ranks. Their strength increased as the war progressed, the two branches being amalgamated in 1863 to form a single Corps of Engineers. Their duties consisted of the construction of fortifications, bridges, roads, siege-works, and map-making, equally vital to the success of an army as the duties of the Ordnance Corps.

Both corps wore full dress uniforms based upon the infantry pattern, with piping, hat-cords, trouser-stripes and chevrons of the corps facing colour: crimson for the Ordnance and yellow for Engineers. The rank of Ordnance Sergeant was distinguished by a crimson star over the normal three-bar chevrons. Hat-badges consisted of a brass grenade for the Ordnance, and a brass castle with regimental and company identification for the Engineers.

Officers' uniforms conformed to the same basic style, but included the following distinctions: the Engineers hat-badge consisted of a wreath of laurel and palm in gold embroidery encircling a silver castle; that of Topographical Engineer officers was a shield surrounded by an oak-leaf wreath, all in gold embroidery.

Officers' shoulder-bars had dark blue backgrounds. Ordnance officers in full dress wore the Staff uniform, with the hat-badge of an exploding grenade in gold embroidery on a black velvet background.

32. U.S.A.: a) Hospital Steward, Full Dress.
b) Lieutenant-Colonel Surgeon, in overcoat.

The Medical Department consisted of only 115 officers at the commencement of the war, of whom twenty-seven resigned upon the outbreak of hostilities, twenty-four forming the nucleus of the Confederate Medical Department. The Union Department was rapidly expanded.

Officers (the army surgeons) wore the Staff uniform, with their own pattern of sword, and the letters 'M.S.' in old English style on the epaulette-straps. Medical Cadets were distinguished by green shoulder-bars, with a half-inch wide strip of gold lace running down the centre. Officers of all branches of the army were permitted (by an order of 22 November 1864) to remove the conspicuous shoulder-bars, provided the rank insignia was embroidered directly onto the coat; this gave official sanction to the attempt by many officers to render themselves less obvious to enemy marksmen. The officer illustrated in this plate wears the regulation officers' braided overcoat.

'Other ranks' of the Medical Department were the Hospital Stewards. In full dress they wore the standard infantry uniform but with crimson trimming and trouser-stripes. Their rank-badge consisted of a 'half chevron' on the sleeve, of emerald green cloth with yellow edging, bearing a badge of a yellow caduceus in the centre. The badge on the 'Hardee' hat consisted of a brass laurel wreath encircling the white metal letters 'U.S.'; hat-cords were of mixed green and buff cord.

Officers of all branches of the Union army wore embroidered cloth badges in place of the brass hat-badge used to hold up the brim of the 'Hardee' hat on occasion; this badge consisted of a black velvet oval with gold thread edge, with the same device embroidered in gold thereon as on the more usual brass hat-badge.

Confederate surgeons (holding the nominal rank of major) wore the standard frock-coat, with black collar and cuffs, black képi and trouser-stripes, gold lace and green sash, their uniform in other ways conforming to the regulation pattern.

33. U.S.A.: a) Private, 4th New Hampshire Regiment.
b) Private, 22nd New York Regiment.
c) Captain, Invalid Corps.

In April 1863 the Invalid Corps was established, consisting of officers and men of the Union army unfit for full combat duty due to injury or illness but who could perform limited infantry service. A total of twenty-four regiments and 188 separate companies were established, who performed guard and garrison duty to relieve front-line soldiers. The name was changed on 18 March 1864 to The Veteran Reserve Corps, as the previous initial of the Invalid Corps coincided with those stamped on worn-out equipment and animals ('Inspected – Condemned'), which had caused some friction within the corps! Officers wore the regulation képi, sky-blue frock-coats with dark blue rank-bars, and sky blue trousers with two dark blue stripes down the seam; other ranks had képis and trousers like the regular army, but sky blue 'jersey jackets cut long in the waist' and trimmed with dark blue. This uniform was extremely unpopular as the members of the Invalid Corps disliked such obvious distinction from the 'real soldiers' fit for active service. Regular troops also were jealous of the Invalids who had easier tasks. Eventually officers of the Veteran Reserve Corps were allowed to wear the normal dark blue frock-coat, and so regain their pride by appearing like front-line troops.

The 4th New Hampshire Infantry wore, for a period, a 'pith helmet' or sun helmet, designed to protect the wearer from the heat of the sun. Such helmets were not uncommon (particularly in the earlier part of the war), and were privately-purchased by many officers as well as being issued to certain regiments. The 22nd New York (Union Greys) wore militia-style grey uniforms with red facings and white piping, the whole uniform being styled to resemble the French type of costume.

34. C.S.A.: a) General, Full

Dress.
b) Major, Engineers,
Full Dress.
c) Brigadier-General.

Confederate General officers wore a frock-coat for full dress, not dissimilar to that of the Federal regulations, but of grey with buff facing-colour on the collar, cuffs and piping. Their buttons were arranged in pairs, eight per row. Rank was indicated by an embroidered badge on either side of the collar, consisting of three stars within a laurel wreath, by cuff-lacing of four thicknesses wide, and by the buff waist-sash. A small bicorn 'chapeau' was authorised for full dress wear, but in practice seems to have been worn even less than its Federal counterpart, plain 'slouch' hats being preferred by the majority; otherwise, a dark blue képi with gold lace decorations four thicknesses wide was worn. Trousers were dark blue with two $\frac{5}{8}$-inch wide stripes of gold lace down the outer seams. Another popular garment was a frock-coat more resembling a civilian overcoat, worn open to expose the waistcoat (this figure is taken from a photograph of G. W. C. Lee). Rank-badges were frequently worn on the turned-back lapels of such coats. As in many other cases, self-designed uniforms or even civilian clothes were far more common on active service than regulation costume.

The Major of Engineers illustrated wears the officially-prescribed full dress uniform with low 'chapeau' with gold star badge on the right-hand side, gold lace band and transverse plume of black ostrich feathers. Facings for the Engineer Corps were buff like those of the Staff, but the sash was red. The buttons on the frock-coat were arranged in the pattern authorised for all except general officers: i.e. single-spaced.

35. C.S.A.: a) Major, Cavalry.
b) General of Cavalry.

Though officially required to wear the regulation frock-coat, many Confederate cavalry officers preferred short jackets, often double-breasted with yellow-lined lapels which could be buttoned back to give the garment an almost eighteenth-century appearance. Collar, cuffs and piping were also in the yellow distinctive colour of the cavalry, with rank badges and cuff-lacing as per regulations. Underneath the jacket was worn any type of waistcoat, shirt and cravat. Officially, the képi was the prescribed headgear, but hats, usually black or grey in colour, were by far the most common form of head-dress. Most officers wore the regulation yellow silk sash, and white or buff gauntlets were very popular. According to regulations, trousers were light blue with a 1¼-inch wide yellow stripe down the outer seam, but grey or other colours were not uncommon, while buff corduroy as illustrated was perhaps the most popular of all. Boots were either of the short ankle-length variety, or the large-topped knee-boots illustrated.

Most Confederate cavalry officers carried a sabre of varying pattern: the version illustrated could be either a captured Federal weapon, a Confederate copy of the same, or a European import: straight-bladed imported weapons were also in common usage. The sword was supported on black leather slings from the waist-belt, which sometimes had an extra support in the form of a narrow shoulder-belt, not unlike the famous British 'Sam Browne' belt adopted later in the century. The pistol was a universal sidearm, that illustrated being a copy of the Colt 'Dragoon' revolver, manufactured by J. H. Dance and Bros. Officers' horse-furniture was much the same as that of the rank and file, or civilian items; ornate shabraques as specified by Federal regulations had few, if any, corresponding items in the Confederate army.

The General officer of cavalry illustrated wears a uniform which is basically of a cavalry style, but with appropriate rank-badges on the collar, and General's cuff-lace and button-arrangement.

36. C.S.A.: Private, Cavalry, Campaign Dress.

This plate shows a typical Confederate trooper of about 1863, before the most severe shortages of uniforms and equipment led to the virtual disappearance of anything resembling regulation styles. Though many militia units had good horse-furniture of pre-war vintage, there was little uniformity in the type of saddle used, varying from the U.S. McClellan pattern or its Confederate copy, the older Grimsley and Jennifer patterns, with numerous imported models and civilian saddles. A large number of Model 1842 and Model 1850 U.S. Dragoon bits were used, as well as numerous imported varieties, but harnessing was in most cases much simpler than that used by the Federals. Saddle-bags were often replaced by small canvas bags or sacks, and any available material served as saddle-blankets. Stirrups were either wooden or, more popularly, heavy cast brass, as well as numerous non-regulation varieties. Bosses and decorations (where they existed at all) were usually of plain brass, though some existed with 'c.s.' or 'c.s.a.' stamped on. Officers frequently used horse-furniture as plain as that of the other ranks.

The trooper illustrated wears a regulation shell-jacket with yellow facings, but with the customary 'slouch' hat replacing the képi. Equipment is carried on the saddle-blanket, rolled greatcoat, canteen and cloth haversack – as was on occasion the sword. The trooper is armed with an imported 'Prussian'-style straight-bladed sabre with brass hilt, and a carbine; pistols were extremely popular and it was not unusual for a shotgun to be carried in place of the carbine.

In the Confederate army, each cavalryman had to provide his own horse, being reimbursed by the Government for every day's service. His mount was only replaced by the Government if killed in action; if the horse died of disease or the hardships of campaign, the trooper had to provide another from his own pocket. If unable to buy, capture or otherwise acquire a replacement, the trooper had to transfer to the infantry, by which system many veteran cavalrymen were lost to the Confederacy.

37. C.S.A.: a) Corporal, Cavalry, Full Dress, with Guidon.
b) Sergeant, 1st Virginia Cavalry.

The regulation cavalry uniform consisted of a double-breasted frock-coat with yellow facings and trimming, and two rows of seven buttons on the breast. N.C.O.s wore yellow chevrons and $1\frac{3}{4}$-inch stripes on the outer seams of their light blue trousers; senior N.C.O.s were officially supposed to wear yellow sashes, but in practice these were almost non-existent. The regulation képi was yellow with a dark blue band. However, very few uniforms conformed to these regulations, the prescribed items being replaced by hats, shell-jackets, double-breasted fatigue-blouses or Federal-style fatigue dress, with or without facings and piping. Musicians were supposed to have yellow lace on the breast but this was seldom (if ever) worn. The corporal illustrated in this plate wears a uniform conforming almost exactly to the official regulations, except the rectangular belt-plate bearing 'c.s.' or 'c.s.a.' has been replaced by a plain brass buckle, a very popular style.

The guidon carried is based upon the first National flag, with a variation in the placement of the stars, six small ones being grouped around a larger one. Other variations existed, including one with seven four-pointed stars arranged in three rows. Many Confederate units carried individual, regimentally-designed standards as in the infantry; the Battle Flag was carried both as a guidon and as a thirty-inch square standard by cavalry units.

The 1st Virginia Cavalry was formed early in 1861 under the command of Major James Ewell Brown ('Jeb') Stuart, a West Point graduate who had served as Lee's A.D.C. during John Brown's raid on Harper's Ferry. By the summer of 1861 the 1st Virginia's strength had increased from four to ten companies. The regiment served with the Army of Northern Virginia throughout the war, performing invaluable reconnaissance duty as well as participating in daring raids into Federal territory; it served at First and Second Bull Run, Fredericksburg and Chancellorsville, at the great cavalry action at Brandy Station, and at Yellow Tavern, where Stuart, one of the finest cavalry leaders to emerge from the war, was killed.

The 1st Virginia was uniformed in 'Hussar' style, their grey shell-jackets being faced and braided with black. Unusually for regiments wearing this type of braid, N.C.O.s' chevrons were yellow. The fashionable long hair, beards and plumed 'slouch' hats gave the regiment a deliberately-acquired 'cavalier' style. Not all the companies wore black shoulder-straps; the regiment was formed from independent units including the Clark County Cavalry, Valley Rangers, Amelia Light Dragoons, Loudoun Light Horse, Albemarle Light Horse, Harrisonburg Cavalry, Howard Dragoons and the Sumter Mounted Guards. Known as 'The Black Horse Cavalry', the 1st Virginia began the war mounted totally on black horses, but replacements being scarce, this

distinction was of short duration (the unit should not be confused with the Black Horse Troop, Company 'H' of the 4th Virginia Cavalry). Throughout his career, Stuart was noted for the black plume he always wore in his hat, like that of the 1st Virginia. The sergeant illustrated is armed with a Federal Sharps' Carbine.

38. C.S.A.: a) Sergeant, 1st Texas Cavalry, 1861.
b) Private, Charleston Light Dragoons, 1860.

Raised from independent volunteer companies in South Carolina, the 4th South Carolina Cavalry (Rutledge Cavalry) contained the Charleston Light Dragoons (Rutledge Rangers), as Company 'K'. The splendid, almost Napoleonic, uniform included the ornate leather and brass dragoon helmet, which bore the State emblem – the Palmetto tree – on a rosette at each side of the helmet, and on the front plate, which being a crescent-shaped device, itself repeated another of the emblems found on the South Carolina flag; the Palmetto tree was also stamped on the waist-belt plate. This magnificent uniform, however, was reserved for full dress occasions, being replaced by grey fatigue uniforms (issued in December 1860) for active service.

The 1st Texas Cavalry (also known as the Texas Mounted Rifles or Partisan Rangers), though uniformed in a basically-regulation style, had black facings on the shell-jackets and the unusual cuff-flaps; as in many other Texan units, the 'Lone Star' device was much in evidence. The 1st Texas served in Fitzburgh Lee's Brigade; it should not be confused with the other Partisan Rangers (5th North Carolina Cavalry), or with Companies 'F' and 'H' of the 2nd Texas Cavalry, both known as the Texas Mounted Riflemen.

The sergeant is illustrated examining a captured Federal regulation-issue 'McClellan' saddle.

39. C.S.A.: a) Private, 26th Texas Cavalry (Debray's Mounted Riflemen).
   b) Private, Texas Cavalry, with Guidon.
   c) Private, 1st Kentucky Cavalry Brigade.

Xavier Blanchard Debray, a graduate of the French military academy of St Cyr, was in the French diplomatic service until his emigration to Texas in 1852. A newspaper publisher in San Antonio before the war, he served as Governor's A.D.C. until commissioned to raise a regiment in Bexar County, with himself as Colonel. The 26th Texas Cavalry, also known as Debray's Mounted Riflemen, was uniformed and armed in a typically French fashion, the regulation cavalry dress having green facings and piping, brass shoulder-scales, and brass numerals '26' on the collars of N.C.O.s and privates. Musicians wore the usual pattern of lacing on the breast, but in the unusual green colour. It is not certain, however, whether this uniform was ever issued to any members of the regiment other than to Debray and his second-in-command. The 26th were armed with Mexican lances with yellow and blue pennons; these were a dubious advantage, and were replaced in October 1862 by Enfield rifles and revolvers. Debray, commissioned Colonel of the 26th Texas on 5 December 1861, rose to the rank of Brigadier-General by April 1864. His regiment served along the Rio Grande and in the Red River Campaign.

The Confederate cavalry greatcoat was double-breasted with standing collar and brass buttons, the cape long enough to reach the cuffs of the coat, the whole being grey in colour. It is doubtful, however, whether many such overcoats conformed exactly to regulations, a wide variety of styles and designs being used. The private illustrated wears the official pattern, and has the distinctive all-yellow képi of the 1st Kentucky Cavalry Brigade.

The Texan cavalryman wears a simple all-grey uniform, the yellow facing colour being born only on the collar; the guidon is the 'Lone Star' State flag, carried in this shape by Texan cavalry units.

The Kentucky cavalryman is shown armed with a Deane and Adams revolver fitted with a Kerr patent ramrod.

40. C.S.A.: a) Private, Georgia Governor's Horse Guard, 1861.
   b) Private, Southern Militia, 1860-61.

The Governor's Horse Guards

(Georgia) wore uniforms based on the popular 'Hussar' style, combining the volunteer grey with the black braiding common to several such corps, the plumed hat, and the unusual white cross-belt. The unit was armed with revolvers and sabres. The Horse Guards formed Company 'A' of the Cavalry Battalion of Phillips's Georgia Volunteer Legion; the infantry detachment of Governor's Guard became Company 'E' of the 3rd Georgia Infantry.

The other figure in this plate (taken from a contemporary photograph) shows the typical Southern militia uniform worn prior to the outbreak of war, and which formed the basis of the Confederate Dress Regulations of 1861.

41. C.S.A.: a) Private, Sussex Light Dragoons, 1861.
   b) Captain, Sussex Light Dragoons, 1861.

The Sussex Light Dragoons wore a most distinctive uniform, their képi being of such a height as to almost qualify for the name 'shako'; of blue cloth with yellow braid, it bore a brass badge of the letters 's.l.d.' over crossed sabres. Officers wore a variation of regulation frock-coat, but considerably longer than usual, and distinguished by a grey collar. Other ranks wore shirts with 'plastron'-style front panels, which may have been reversible to show a yellow panel for full dress. Trousers for all ranks were dark blue. The corps was armed with the usual weapons – sabre and revolver.

A number of Virginia-raised cavalry units bore the title 'Sussex'; as in many other cases, the lineage of volunteer companies is complicated: for example, one corps of Sussex Cavalry (also known as the Sussex Jackson Avengers) was orginally Captain B. F. Winfield's company of the 16th Battalion Virginia Cavalry, later becoming Company 'D' of the 13th Virginia Cavalry; another Sussex Cavalry was Company 'H' of the 13th Virginia; while Company 'C' of the 5th Virginia Cavalry was known as either the Sussex Light Dragoons or Sussex Cavalry. Both the 5th Virginia (Company 'E') and the 13th Virginia ('G') included companies known as Surry Cavalry, the latter originally forming part of the 16th Bn. Virginia Cavalry. The problem is further complicated by the existence of a corps known as the Sussex Riflemen (Company 'E', 16th Virginia Infantry)!

42. C.S.A.: a) 1st Lieutenant, Hampton's Legion.
   b) 1st Sergeant, Beaufort Troop.

Soon after the State's secession, Wade Hampton, an immensely rich and aristocratic South Carolina plantation owner, raised (largely at his own expense) a volunteer 'legion' with an original strength of six infantry companies, four cavalry companies, and a battery of artillery equipped with six English Blakely fieldpieces, purchased from Hampton's own pocket. There was no difficulty in raising recruits – more than twice the required number volunteered. In common with many other volunteer corps, each company preserved its identity and its own uniforms for a time; in the Legion's infantry battalion for example, company names were as follows: 'A' Washington Light Infantry, 'B' Watson Guards, 'C' Manning Guards, 'D' Gist Rifles, 'E' Bozeman Guards, 'F' Davis Guards, 'G' Claremont Rifles, 'H' South Carolina Zouave Volunteers.

This plate illustrates two variations on the cavalry uniform worn within the Legion; both are of the 'Hussar' style, with loops of braid on the breast. The 1st Lieutenant's uniform is marked by the absence of sleeve-lace, but retains the cavalry facing colour. The Beaufort District Troop (or Dragoons), company 'C' of the Legion's Cavalry detachment, was uniformed in a more sombre style with black facings, lace and hat-plume. Both figures are shown armed in the popular Confederate fashion, with a brace of revolvers in place of the sabre. Other cavalry companies retained their individuality within the Legion: for example, Company 'A' was known as Brook's Dragoons or the Edgefield Hussars, and Company 'D' the Congaree Troop.

Wade Hampton led his Legion with distinction at First Bull Run (where he was wounded), succeeded to the command of Stuart's cavalry corps and rose to the rank of Major-General, becoming Governor of South Carolina after the war and eventually senator. The Legion itself became part of Longstreet's Division in November 1861, and was eventually split up after the Peninsular campaign, the cavalry joining Rosser's Regiment, the infantry becoming part of Hood's Texas Brigade, and the artillery becoming Hart's South Carolina Battery.

43. C.S.A.: 8th Texas Cavalry.
a) Private, Campaign Dress.
b) Private, Regulation Dress.

The Texas Rangers were originally raised during the War of Texan Independence as a quasi-military mobile police force to protect the settlers from the depredations of marauding Indians. Reorganised by Sam Houston, the Ranger companies acted as State Militia during the Civil War, but their name was transferred to the 8th Texas Cavalry, raised by B. F. Terry and Thomas S. Lubbock, generally known as the 1st Texas Rangers or 'Terry's Texas Rangers'.

Officially, the uniform consisted of grey képi with yellow band, light grey shell-jacket with yellow facings, and dark grey trousers with yellow stripe down the outer seam. The rigours of campaigning and the shortages of material compelled the regiment to dress in whatever clothing they could find or steal – captured Federal items, black or grey 'slouch' hat, coloured scarf; brown, grey or blue jackets with or without red facings; trousers of any colour, many captured from the Union; in fact any item of clothing was pressed into service, being given 'uniformity' by the addition of scarlet trimming when possible. Wearing such costume had its dangers: on 5 January 1864 Private

E. S. Dodd of the 8th Texas was shot by the Union as a spy, having been captured wearing items of Federal uniform! As popular with most Texan units, the 'Lone Star' emblem of the State was always in evidence on belt-plates, accoutrements and head-dress; Company 'F', in fact, was known as the 'Lone Star Rangers'.

Serving in the West, the 8th Texas had a fine record, and in the 1870's the Texas Rangers were re-organised as a police force to patrol and protect against bandits and Indians; they continue as an independent police force to the present day, maintaining the high record of their forebears. The 8th Texas Cavalry should not be confused with other units bearing the same title: Rosser's Texas Mounted Rangers (Company 'K', 10th Virginia Cavalry), or with various units of 'Texas Rangers': 'E', 2nd Texas Cavalry; 'K', 8th Texas Cavalry; and 'F', 59th Virginia Infantry.

44. C.S.A.: a) Major, Infantry, Full Dress.
b) Colonel, 20th Alabama Regiment.
c) 2nd Lieutenant, Infantry, Campaign Dress.

In full dress, Confederate infantry officers wore the regulation frock-coat with light blue facings and trimming, though all-grey uniforms were not uncommon. Rank-lacing on the cuffs and rank-badges on the collar were of gold lace; buttons were gilt. The képi was officially light blue with dark blue band and gold lace, though it appeared in a combination of light and dark · blue and grey as well. Trousers were light blue with a 1¾-inch dark blue stripe; rank was further distinguished by the red silk sash worn under the waistbelt.

On campaign, the uniform frequently underwent radical alteration: though the frock-coat was retained in many cases, shorter jackets like those worn by the rank and file were popular. The képi was frequently replaced by a 'slouch' hat, commonly black, with or without decorative feather plumes. Trousers were often grey or blue-grey, sometimes worn with knee-boots as illustrated. The sash was frequently discarded, and often a pistol alone was carried, the sword not being universally popular. Overcoats, when used, were like those of the other ranks, though numerous non-regulation styles existed.

The officer of the 20th Alabama Infantry illustrated (based upon a contemporary photograph) wears the standard infantry uniform, with the addition of felt hat with turned-up brim. Isham W. Garrott, Colonel of the 20th, was promoted Brigadier-General (28 May 1863); he was killed by a sharpshooter at Vicksburg on 17 June 1863.

The 2nd Lieutenant illustrated is armed with an ornate, pearl-handled Navy Colt revolver.

45. C.S.A.: a) Private, Infantry, Full Dress.
b) Sergeant-Major, Infantry, Full Dress.

This plate shows the regulation full

dress of enlisted men of the Confederate infantry, though it is doubtful whether many were ever issued (if at all); it is possible that the uniform never went beyond the prototype stage, as materials ran short after the opening months of the war. Even if some were issued, it is probable that only officers wore a uniform completely in accordance with dress regulations.

According to the manual 'Uniforms and Dress of the Army of the Confederate States' issued in September 1861 by Adjutant- and Inspector-General Samuel Cooper, it is possible that the regulation head-dress was intended to be a shako similar to the 1851 pattern of the U.S. Army, possibly of black, dark blue or grey cloth, with pompom and presumably brass plate; however, the regulations are so vague that the pattern of shako or whatever cannot be determined and in any case 'General Order No. 4' of January 1862 authorised the use of the forage cap (képi) to be worn by all ranks in full dress, the top to be light blue, with a dark blue band.

The grey frock-coat was to extend half-way between the knees and hips, double-breasted, with two rows of seven buttons and light blue facings and piping; N.C.O.s' rank chevrons and sashes (the latter worn when the sword was carried) were to be of the light blue distinguishing colour also. Trousers were to be light blue, with a 1¼-inch dark blue stripe for N.C.O.s; musicians were to have Federal-style light blue frogging on the breast of the coat, and a light blue sash. All equipment was to be of black leather. The brass infantry badge (a hunting horn) was officially to be worn on the top of the képi (similar badges were authorised for other branches – crossed sabres for cavalry, crossed cannon-barrels for artillery), and, if possible, the regimental number on the front of the cap; but it seems extremely unlikely that any of these devices were ever actually worn.

46. C.S.A.: Private, Infantry, Service Dress.

This plate illustrates two versions of the semi-regulation service uniform worn by the rank and file of the Confederate infantry, before the shortages of material led to the complete degeneration of uniform into semi-civilian and home-dyed costume.

The authorised fatigue uniform consisted of a grey double-breasted, blouse with two rows of seven buttons but it seems likely that the single-breasted version illustrated was more common. This uniform was worn with or without light blue facings, and occasionally 'slash'-type cuffs were worn in place of the authorised pointed variety. Trousers were the regulation light blue, sometimes captured from the Federals.

Before the wearing of the brimmed hat became almost universal, the colouring of the képi was changed to grey with a band of light blue, and all-grey képis were not uncommon. As supplies became scarcer, the fatigue coat was often replaced by a grey shell-jacket, often worn without any facings, or with just the collar of light blue. Grey trousers were worn with or without a light blue stripe down the outer seams. Equipment, originally of black leather, gradually became brown or 'natural' in colour as black dye became scarcer. Much Federal equipment was captured and pressed into service, a favourite trick being to wear the Union waist-belt with the 'U.S.' plate upside-down.

47. C.S.A.: a) Private, Infantry.
b) Private, Infantry.
c) Private, Company 'B', 15th Virginia Infantry.

This plate shows the regulation double-breasted overcoat and elbow-length cape with standing collar. Greatcoats of completely regulation pattern were scarce, numerous semi-regulation styles being the most common. One of the privates illustrated wears a regulation képi (complete with regimental number on the front, an ornament frequently not issued); the other wears a home made cloth or woollen cap, and a knitted 'muffler'.

Company·'B' of the 15th Virginia Infantry, the 'Virginia Life Guard', wore uniforms made at the Crenshaw Woollen Mills of Richmond, Virginia, consisting of a blue flannel 'hunting shirt' with blue fringes, blue cap, black trousers and white gloves. This was an unusual variation on the usual type of volunteer uniform.

48. C.S.A.: a) Corporal, Infantry, with 1st National Flag.
b) Private, Infantry, with Battle Flag.

The corporal illustrated wears an all-grey Federal-style fatigue uniform of Confederate grey, with only the chevrons in the infantry distinctive colour, and knapsack replaced by a green civilian blanket. His colour is the First National Flag of the Confederacy (adopted 4 March 1861), known as the 'Stars and Bars' from the three large stripes and from the seven white stars arranged in a circle on the blue canton. There were numerous variations on this design, the number and arrangement of stars varying considerably, with sometimes as many as fourteen stars arranged in lines on the canton.

The private is notable because he wears not a single item of regulation equipment, a common state of affairs as the war moved into its later stages and materials became progressively more scarce. The straw hat, unbleached cotton shirt, neckerchief and 'natural' leather belts are all civilian items, while the trousers and 'gum blanket' shoulder-roll are captured Union items. The pistol carried is a Starr .44 revolver. The Confederate Battle Flag as illustrated consisted of a dark blue saltaire cross on a red field, edged white, the cross bearing thirteen white stars. Officially four feet square, the Battle Flag existed in larger and smaller versions, and other designs based upon the pattern were not unknown – a blue flag with white cross, or a white flag with blue cross and white stars, for example. Regimental titles and battle-honours were often inscribed upon the Battle Flag as well as upon the central white stripe of the First National Flag.

Confederate colour-bearers were (according to regulations) to wear a badge of crossed flags on the arm to signify their appointment, but due to the high casualty-rate among colour-parties in many cases not only this badge but also the colour-belt was not worn.

Considerable confusion resulted in battle due to the similarity of the First National Flag to the United States flag, so a new National Flag was designed and adopted on 1 May 1863, this consisting of an all-white flag, twice as long as it was deep, with the Battle Flag (or 'Southern Cross') in the top canton nearest the pole. Even this design was not satisfactory, as it could easily be mistaken for a flag of surrender, so on 4 March 1865 the Third National Flag was adopted, this being basically the same design as the Second, but not as long and with a vertical red bar at the end furthest from the pole; but this design was never used in battle – it was flown only briefly over Richmond before the war ended.

Confederate regiments, even more than their Union counterparts, carried a varied assortment of standards – the designs might include National Flag, State Flag, any number of Battle Flags and independent company or regimental flags – all within the same unit!

49. C.S.A.: a) Sergeant, Texas Infantry, with State Flag, 1863.
b) Sergeant-Major, South Carolina Volunteers, with State Flag, 1861.
Many Confederate units carried the Flags of their native State; two such are illustrated in this plate. The South Carolina flag, with blue background bearing the State emblems of Crescent moon and Palmetto tree, was that finally adopted on secession; prior to this (1860–61), South Carolina units carried a red flag bearing a dark blue cross with vertical and horizontal arms; at the intersection of the arms was a large white star. On each of the horizontal arms were four smaller stars, and three on each of the vertical arms; the crescent and Palmetto tree appeared in white in the upper canton nearest the pole.

Texan units, proud of their sobriquet 'Lone Star State', carried the familiar Texan flag. Other State banners varied considerably: Virginian units, for example, carried a blue flag bearing the State seal in the centre; the North Carolina design was like that of Texas, but with a white star on a red bar, and white over blue stripes. Arkansas units often carried Battle Flags of a plain white cross on blue field. Many corps also carried 'regimental' banners of their own design, often bearing patriotic mottoes: for example, the flag of the Fayetteville Independent Light Infantry (Company 'H' 1st North Carolina Infantry) bore the words 'He That Hath No Stomach For This Fight, Let Him Depart', whilst that of the Florida Independent Blues (Company 'E' 3rd Florida Infantry) bore, on a blue background, seven white stars over three white cotton-bolls with green leaves, over the white letters 'Any Fate But Submission'.

The South Carolinan sergeant-major wears a uniform typical of those of the early volunteer corps, consisting of shell-jacket, képi and trousers, of plain grey with light blue chevrons and sash. The belt-plate bears the Palmetto Tree emblem; the regulation shoulder-belt to support the butt of the colour-pole was worn over one shoulder. The Texan sergeant also wears the State emblem, having the 'Lone Star' badge on hat and belt-plate. The fashion of wearing the shell-jacket fastened by only one button at the neck, hanging open to expose the shirt, was a very popular style.

50. C.S.A.: a) Private, Sumter Light Guard.
b) Bass Drummer, Sumter Light Guard.
c) Officer, Sumter Light Guard.

The figures on this plate are based upon a photograph taken in April 1861 of the Sumter Light Guard (Company 'K', 4th Georgia Volunteers); being in black and white, it is difficult to be precise as to the exact colouring of the uniforms. The company wore dark uniforms (képi, shell-jacket and trousers) with light-coloured shoulder-straps and trouser-stripes, officers being distinguished by frock-coats, sashes, knee-boots and the broad white shoulder-belt. Equipment appears to have been of standard Federal pattern, though it is likely that some form of State device was worn upon the belt-plates. The drummer appears to be wearing an almost civilian-style 'uniform', with large bow-tie and shirt-collar visible beneath the turned-back lapels of the jacket, and a remarkably battered felt hat turned up at the front.

Other details (common to many Confederate volunteer corps) are shown on the photograph but not illustrated. Shirt-collars and even ties show above the shell-jacket collars of many of the rank and file, and not a few have unholstered pistols tucked into their waist-belts. The company colour-bearer has a broad black shoulder-belt to carry the colour-pole, the flag itself being of the First National Flag design, with six white stars arranged around a seventh star in the blue canton. N.C.O.s' chevrons are the same colour as the shoulder-straps and trouser-stripes. The company 'band', in addition to the drummer illustrated, consisted of a side-drummer and fifer, the former carrying his drum on a black leather shoulder-belt. Both musicians are wearing not the usual képi, but 'pork-pie' style of fatigue caps like the pattern worn in the U.S.–Mexican War; in other respects, they are dressed like the privates.

51. C.S.A.: a) Private, Company 'E', 23rd Virginia Volunteers, Service Dress.
b) Private, ditto, Full Dress.
c) Private, Savannah Volunteer Guard, Full Dress.

The Booklyn Greys were organised at Brooklyn, Halifax County, Virginia, and in May 1861 were designated Company 'E' of the 23rd Virginia Volunteers. Other companies which composed this regiment were the Amelia Greys, Amelia Rifles, Anthony Greys, Blue Stone Greys, Louisa Greys, Louisa Rifles, Prince Edward Central Guards, Richmond Sharpshooters and the Warwick Rangers. The uniform of the Brooklyn Greys consisted of a tall képi of grey with a black or dark blue band bearing the letters 'B.G.' in brass; the képi is also shown covered with a black 'waterproof'. The grey frock-coats were trimmed with black or dark blue braid, the collars being cut open to expose the neck, or shirt-collar and tie if worn; collar-loops were of yellow or gold braid, one or two loops being worn at each side. Trousers were grey with similar trimming, and leather equipment seems to have been white with oval brass plates, or black with brass buckles.

One of the more elaborately-dressed volunteer corps, the Savannah City Light Guard formed Company 'D' of the 1st Georgia Volunteers and later, variously titled the Savannah Guards, Savannah Volunteers or Savannah Volunteer Guard, served in the 18th Battalion Georgia Infantry. The elaborate uniform no doubt gave way almost immediately to a more regulation-style fatigue uniform, or at least the epaulettes would have been removed and the shako replaced by a képi. Officers probably wore a similar costume, with normal badges of rank. The unit should not be confused with a company of boys also known as the

Savannah Volunteer Guards (Captain W. G. Charlton's company of Georgia volunteers), nor with the Savannah River Guards (Company 'K', 3rd South Carolina Cavalry).

52. C.S.A.: a) **Private, Maryland Guard Zouaves.**
b) **Private, Company 'A', 5th Georgia Regiment, Service Dress.**
c) **Private, ditto, Full Dress.**

Dressed in typical Zouave fashion, the Maryland Guard Zouaves had a chequered career: originally Company 'H' of the 47th Virginia Infantry, they became 'E' of the 1st Battalion Maryland Infantry, and afterwards became 'E' of the 2nd Maryland Infantry. Serving at First Bull Run and Gettysburg, they formed part of Brigadier-General George H. 'Maryland' Steuart's Brigade.

The Clinch Rifles formed Company 'A' of the 5th Georgia Infantry, which included other volunteer companies (for example the Griffin Light Guards and the Hardee Rifles), almost all of whom wore different designs of uniform. When in garrison in Pensacola, Florida, General Braxton Bragg nicknamed the corps 'The Pound Cake Regiment' from the varying uniforms of its companies! The Clinch Rifles wore a uniform in the colouring normally associated with the Union army – dark blue képi and frock-coat and light blue trousers – which was a colour-scheme adopted by a number of militia companies of the southern states prior to the war. The cap-badge consisted of the letters 'C.R.' surrounded by a laurel wreath, all in white embroidery. Their uniform was almost identical to that of another Georgia militia corps, the Republican Blues of Savannah, Georgia (later Companies 'B' and 'C', 1st Georgia Volunteers).

Also shown in this plate is a uniform of a member of the company on active service (taken from a contemporary photograph); for coolness and comfort, in summer the frock-coat and képi were replaced in camp by a plain shirt and panama hat. Similar dress was worn by most regiments. The photograph mentioned shows that the Clinch Rifles' camp equipment (tents, canvas buckets, etc.) were all painted with the large letters 'C.R.'.

The 5th Georgia served at Murfreesboro, Chickamauga (suffering 55 per cent casualties) and Gettysburg, and continued in the field after the surrender at Appomattox, under General Edmund Kirby Smith, only finally laying down its arms on 26 April 1865 at Greensboro, North Carolina. The company should not be confused with the Clinch Cavaliers (Company 'G', 11th Georgia State Guards), the Clinch Mountain Boomers ('K', 48th Virginia Infantry), the Clinch Rangers (Georgia), or the Clinch Volunteers ('G' 50th Georgia Infantry).

53. C.S.A.: a) Private, Alexandria Rifles.
b) Private, Woodis Rifles, Full Dress.
c) Drum Major, 1st

Virginia Volunteers, Full Dress.

A militia company raised in Norfolk, Virginia, in 1858, the Woodis Rifles were named after a mayor of the city, Hunter Woodis. Originally forming part of the 3rd Battalion, 54th Virginia Militia, they were called out on 18 April 1861 and designated Company 'C' of the 6th Virginia Regiment upon that unit's organisation. From the Seven Days Battle in 1862, the Woodis Rifles were in continual action until the surrender at Appomattox, notably distinguishing themselves in action. Their uniform was one of the most magnificent of the period, consisting of frock-coat of 'hunting green' with black velvet facings, gilt buttons and much gold lace. The initials of the name, 'W.R.' was repeated on the hat-badge and belt-plate. It is doubtful whether the uniform was ever replaced once the original had worn out: in all probability more regulation uniforms would be adopted. The company maintained an equally impressive band, which was not surprisingly adopted as the regimental band of the 6th Virginia.

The Alexandria Rifles (6th Battalion Virginia Volunteers) also wore green uniforms, but with the more sombre trimming of black lace. These colours were appropriate for a 'rifle' unit: they were the traditional semi-camouflaged colours of European skirmisher corps.

Each company of the 1st Virginia maintained its own distinctive uniform for a period, until a more mundane service uniform was adopted. Field officers wore dark blue frock-coats and trousers, Virginia State buttons, and the 'Hardee' hat. Sergeant-Major Pohlé, Drum-Major of the 1st Virginia Volunteers, came from a Richmond militia company known as the Virginia Rifles, having served in a U.S. Navy band before the war. Pohlé's magnificent uniform, which would hardly have been out of place in Napoleonic France, was reserved for full dress only. The 1st Virginia's regimental band consisted of thirteen musicians, plus a Corps of Drums of fourteen boys aged sixteen or over; both were disbanded upon the reorganisation of the regiment a year after its inception.

54. C.S.A.: Privates, Louisiana Tiger Zouaves.

Chatham Roberdeau ('Rob') Wheat led a varied career; son of an Episcopal minister, he served in the U.S.–Mexican War at the age of twenty, after which he settled in New Orleans as a criminal lawyer. The call of adventure being too strong, he went to South America as a mercenary, finally being commissioned in the Mexican army. Seeking fresh fields, he joined the English Volunteers of Garibaldi's army in Italy, but returned to America upon the outbreak of war. He raised a unit mostly from Irish 'roughs' in New Orleans, officially known as Wheat's Special Battalion or the Louisiana Zouaves, but glorying in the nickname 'Tigers'.

As Major commanding the 'Tigers', Wheat alone could control the unruly elements from which the corps was composed. He led them at First Bull Run where he was shot through both lungs; told that the wound was mortal, he replied 'I don't feel like dying yet', and indeed survived to lead his tough battalion in the Valley campaign. After his mortal wound at Gaines' Mill, the 'Tigers' were never again an effective fighting unit when deprived of Wheat's leadership and discipline.

The Louisiana 'Tigers' wore a typical Zouave costume, consisting of red stocking-cap with blue tassel, dark brown jacket with red braid in varying patterns, red shirts and sashes, and trousers made from bed-ticking, sometimes white with blue stripes or mixtures of red, white and blue. Also known as the 1st Louisiana Special Battalion, the 'Tigers' included the following exotically-named companies: Walker Guards ('A'), Tiger Rifles ('B'), Delta Rangers ('C'), Catahoula Guerrillas or Old Dominion Guards ('D'), and the Wheat Life Guards ('E'). The battalion formed part of the 1st Louisiana Brigade, consisting also of the 6th and 8th Louisiana Regiments and The Pelican Regiment (7th Louisiana); the entire brigade adopted the nickname of Wheat's corps, calling themselves the 'Louisiana Tigers'.

An unofficial addition to the 'Tigers' uniforms were patriotic mottos inscribed upon their stocking-caps or straw hats, for example 'Tigers Win Or Die', 'Tigers Always', or 'Tigers!'

**55. C.S.A.: 1st Battalion
Louisiana Zouaves.
a) Private.
b) 1st Lieutenant.**

The Louisiana Zouave Battalion was raised from Europeans in New Orleans, and wore a typical Zouave-style costume; the main difference between the uniforms of the officers and men was in the style of jacket, the rank and file having proper 'Zouave' sleeved waistcoats, while the officers had a type of shell-jacket with standing collar, bearing the rank markings on the cuffs and collar. The regiment was nicknamed 'The Pelicans' from the design of the State seal often borne upon the waist-belt. The regiment served throughout the war, maintaining a fine record.

Several other Louisiana units bore the name 'Pelicans': the Pelican Greys (Company 'A' 2nd Louisiana Infantry), the Pelican Guards (Infantry Company 'B', Louisiana Legion), the Pelican Rangers ('D' and 'H', 3rd Louisiana), and the Pelican Rifles ('A' 2nd Louisiana, 'K' 3rd Louisiana).

**56. C.S.A.: a) Private,
McClellan's
Zouaves.
b) Private, Chichester
Zouave Cadets.
c) Cadet, Virginia
Military Institute.**

Both Zouave units illustrated in this plate were raised in Charleston, South Carolina. Little is known about the organisation of McClellan's Zouaves, though the corps might have had some connection to Captain C. E.

Chichester's volunteer company of Zouave Cadets who garrisoned Castle Pinckney when it held Federal prisoners after Bull Run. The uniforms of both corps were similar in style, consisting of grey jackets and trousers with red facings; the Zouave Cadets also wore tan leggings in their winter uniform. The belt-plates bore the state devices of Palmetto tree and the letters 's.c.' ('South Carolina'), the Palmetto tree being repeated on the crown of the képis. Officers apparently wore uniforms of regulation cut, but in the regimental colouring.

When the cadets of the Virginia Military Institute were called out to the Battle of Newmarket, they wore a simple fatigue uniform consisting of 'coarse sheep's-gray jacket and trousers' and képi, with the simple equipment illustrated.

**57. C.S.A.: 4th Texas Volunteers:
a) Sergeant,
Company 'B'.
b) Private,
Company 'H'.
c) Private,
Company 'A'.**

The 4th Texas Volunteers were organised in October 1861 at 'Camp Texas' near Richmond, Virginia, from the volunteer companies which had arrived from Texas, command of the regiment going to Colonel John Bell Hood, later promoted to General. Including volunteer companies named the Austin City Light Infantry, the Mustang Greys and the Grimes County Greys, the plate illustrates the uniforms of three companies: the Hardeman Rifles ('A'), the Tom Green Rifles ('B'), and the Porter Guards ('H').

The uniform worn by all three consisted of a basic all-grey fatigue style uniform, with certain company distinctions: the Hardeman Rifles wore grey or black 'slouch 'hats, the Porter Guards grey képis, and the Tom Green Rifles grey slouch-hats and black braid trimming on the jacket and trousers, N.C.O.s' chevrons being of the same black braid. Black leather equipment was worn by all companies, the 'Lone Star' device being commonly displayed on the belt-plates and sometimes (unofficially) as a hat-badge. The sergeant illustrated is further distinguished from the other ranks by a crimson waist-sash.

58. C.S.A.: 3rd Texas Infantry:
a) Private,
Campaign Dress.
b) Corporal,
Campaign Dress.

This plate shows the beginning of the degeneration of the Confederate field uniform, as regulation dress began to wear out and replacements – due to the Federal blockade – became increasingly more scarce. 'Slouch' hats of all colours and descriptions replaced the képi (this being a habit among the troops rather than because of any shortages), and other items of uniform became increasingly less common, civilian clothes, captured Federal items and home-dyed garments appearing in their stead. Confederate soldiers – notably improvident on campaign – discarded

the regulation equipment as being an unnecessary encumberance, replacing it with a rolled blanket or any length of cloth, worn over one shoulder, containing personal possessions and items of spare clothing (where these existed). The canteen shown, of a flat, uncovered tin design, was of the type supplied by Schnitzler and Kirshblower, being stamped with the state name in large letters.

As a previously-independent republic, Texans considered themselves as different from the remaining Confederate states, which probably explains why the 'Lone Star' device was often prominently displayed (unofficially) on pouches and head-dress, as well as on the State belt-plates. These star badges were made of cloth, sewn on to the hat or garment, or of metal, some commercially-produced and purchased by the troops, and often home-made, sometimes converted from silver dollars.

59. C.S.A.: Infantry in
'Butternut', 1865.

As the Confederacy declined and the Federal blockade tightened, the Confederate uniform underwent a gradual change in colour from grey to that illustrated in this plate. Once the supply of grey cloth had run out, the material was dyed with 'butternut' (nut-shells and rust being a common concoction) which produced an endless variety of brown, buff and light khaki shades. This dress, often combined with captured Federal items and pieces of civilian clothing, was in a way a rudimentary form of camouflage, and led to the nickname of

'Butternuts' being bestowed upon the Confederate troops by the Federals. As early as 1862 this type of dress was in use: Union reports spoke of hundreds of Confederate dead at South Mountain (14 September 1862) dressed in 'coarse butternut-colored uniforms . . . very ugly in appearance but well calculated to conceal them from our troops . . .'. It is possible that some Southern militia units were so dressed even before the outbreak of war. The miserable, ragged company which ended the war in 1865 bore little resemblance to the finely-dressed volunteers who had begun it.

The two 'uniforms' illustrated are taken from contemporary photographs; both men wear battered felt hats and ragged, patched clothing. The fashion of wearing the trousers tucked into the socks was very popular in both armies. The equipment was reduced to a minimum, generally consisting of only haversack, canteen and tin mug, the remainder having been thrown away, lost, or never issued. Cartridge-pouches were rarely used, it being easier to carry the cartridges loose in the pockets. Leather equipment was often issued in 'natural' or brown colouring when the supply of black dye ran out. One of the men illustrated has a captured Federal 'gum blanket', the rubber-muslin 'poncho' being used as a shoulder-roll to contain what would not fit into the haversack. After late 1862 the shortage of shoes in the Confederate army was desperate; leather was scarce or unavailable, so in many cases 'utility' or substitute shoes being made: those illustrated are of the type made by nailing leather onto a wooden sole, with old horse-shoes fastened underneath as boot-irons. Other inventions included shoes made of felt (!), gumwood and (in Florida), shoes made of the weed 'kip-leather', claimed by the inventor to be equal to the best French leather. Old saddles and Palmetto-stalks were other ingredients.

60. C.S.A.: Artillery:
a) Captain, Full Dress.
b) Gunner, Service Dress.

Confederate Artillery uniforms supposedly conformed to the regulation style worn by other branches of the army, with the red distinguishing colour worn on the képi, facings and trimming. In practice, however, it is possible that few enlisted men ever wore the prescribed frock-coat, a variety of non-regulation styles being worn on active service.

The officer in this plate wears the regulation uniform; on campaign, brimmed felt hats and short jackets were more commonly used. The gunner is shown in a red-piped shell-jacket, which uniform (taken from contemporary information) was just one of a myriad of styles used even within the same company. One gunner of each team also carried a large leather haversack used to convey cartridges from limber or ammunition-waggon to cannon, providing that there was time and opportunity to obey the conventional drill. Another member of the team carried a combined sponge and rammer, which fulfilled the dual rôle of ramming down the charge and swabbing out the cannon-barrel to clear the bore of any fouled, burnt powder.

61. C.S.A.: a) 2nd Lieutenant, Washington Artillery.
b) Officer, 'A' Battery, 1st Tennessee Light Artillery (Rutledge's Battery).

Organised in 1838 as the 'Native American' Battery (Company 'A' of Persifal Smith's Regiment) and serving in the U.S.–Mexican War, the Washington Artillery of New Orleans was reorganised in 1852. Composed entirely of wealthy citizens of New Orleans, it was said of the militia company that 'At the outbreak of the Civil War there was not a finer organization of citizen soldiery in America'. The corps received much of its equipment from the seizure of Baton Rouge Arsenal on 11 April 1861, including six 6-pounder cannon. Its four companies offered their services to the Confederate government on 26 May 1861, a fifth company being added next day. Four companies served at First Bull Run, the fifth distinguishing itself at Shiloh as part of J. P. Anderson's Brigade. The battalion fought in every action of the Army of Northern Virginia, and after the war gained permission to form the Washington Artillery Veterans Charitable and Benevolent Association; in the regular service, the Washington Artillery sent a battery to the Cuban war and won further honours in both World Wars.

The corps wore dark blue uniforms, officers having frock-coats and other ranks shell-jackets; the red artillery distinguishing colour was borne on képi and on the trimming of the uniform. The rank and file wore pipe-clayed leather belts, their head-dress bearing crossed cannon-barrel badges with the letters 'w.a.', all in brass. Other Confederate artillery units also bearing the name 'Washington Artillery' were Captain G. H. Walter's company of South Carolina Artillery, Company 'A' of the Hampton Legion, Captain P. W. Bibb's company of Tennessee Artillery, the Washington or Hampton Artillery (originally Company 'K' of the 32nd Virginia Infantry, later 'A' of the 1st Virginia Artillery), and the Washington Mounted Artillery ('A', 7th-Battalion South Carolina Infantry).

Rutledge's Battery was raised in Nashville, Tennessee; after its muster in May 1861 it became 'A' Battery of the 1st Tennessee Light Artillery, its commander, Captain A. M. Rutledge, later being assigned to General Polk's staff. The battery supplied its own guns – four 6-pounder smoothbore cannon and two 12-pounder howitzers, cast in a Nashville foundry. In action at Mill Springs and Shiloh, the battery's losses at the latter engagement were so heavy that it was found necessary to amalgamate it with McClure's Battery. The uniform, basically conforming to regulations with red facings; the battery distinguishing letter, 'A', was borne on the collar, and the crossed cannon-barrels device on the hat and shoulder-straps. The unit should not be confused with the Rutledge Horse Artillery (Company 'G', 7th South Carolina Cavalry).

62. C.S.A.: a) Private, Rifle Volunteers.
b) Private, Palmetto Guards.
c) Private, Infantry Volunteers.

The figures illustrated in this plate (taken from contemporary photographs and engravings) show typical volunteer and militia uniforms worn in the early months of the Civil War by the Confederacy. One uniform is based upon a much earlier style, including a flat-topped forage cap covered with black 'waterproof' as worn during the U.S.–Mexican War, and braided shell-jacket. The rifleman wears a leather 'hunting shirt', a traditionally-American garment worn by 'backwoodsmen' and pioneers for more than a century prior to the Civil War.

The Palmetto Guards (South Carolina) uniform is based upon a photograph of Edmund Ruffin, a prominent agriculturist and author, and an ardent secessionist. Ruffin (1794–1865) claimed to have fired the first shots at both Fort Sumter and First Bull Run; his claim of having fired the first shot of the war seems a dubious one, though it is possible that he fired the first shot from Steven's Battery on Cummings Point after Captain James had fired the signal gun. Ruffin shot himself on 15 June 1865 'because he was unwilling to live under the U.S. Government'. The

Palmetto Guards appear to have worn a civilian-style suit, with the addition of military equipment and hat. The hat had an upturned brim on the right-hand side, with the letters 'P.G.' and a laurel wreath on the front; another small badge (probably the state emblem) was worn on the left-hand side. Two companies of South Carolina troops bore the title 'Palmetto Guards': Company 'I' of the 2nd S.C. Infantry, and 'A' of the 18th Battalion, S.C. Siege Artillery. The same name was also used by Company 'C' of the 19th Georgia Infantry.

The rifleman is armed with a custom-built, heavy-barrelled sniper's rifle, with brass telescopic sight running the length of the barrel, and a 'set' trigger. Used in small numbers, principally by the Federals, these weapons, in the hands of trained sharpshooters, produced feats of scarcely credible accuracy.

63. U.S.A.: a) Commander, U.S. Navy, Summer Campaign Dress, 1862.
b) Captain, U.S. Navy, Undress, 1862.

U.S. Navy full dress uniforms for officers included a bicorn hat, worn with the frock-coat; its use, however was as restricted as that of its Army counterpart, the dress illustrated being the most common wear on service. Until 1862, only the ranks of captain, commander and lieutenant existed; all wore the frock-coat and peaked cap, rank being indicated by

¾-inch wide bands of gold lace, the lieutenant wearing one, commander two and captain three. To accommodate the rapid expansion of the navy during the war, the ranks of lieutenant-commander, commodore and admiral were re-created in 1862, and a new system of rank-marking devised in 1863, with several varieties of wide and narrow bands of lace being worn during the intervening period without much co-ordination. Rank badges worn prior to 1862 were as follows: Captain – shoulder-bars like those of the Army, blue cloth ground, gold lace border, silver rank-badges of eagle and anchor in centre; 1½-inch gold lace band around cap, cap-badge of silver eagle and anchor in an oak and laurel wreath. Flag Officers (senior Captain, Squadron-commanders) – as Captain, but silver star at ends of shoulder-bars. Commanders – as Captain, but badges of silver crossed fouled anchors on shoulder-bars and inside cap-wreath. Lieutenants – as Captain, but one silver anchor on shoulder-bars and cap. Other officers had no lace on their sleeves, their rank markings being: Master – plain shoulder-bars, cap-badge as Lieutenant. Passed Midshipman – gold lace shoulder-bars, cap-badge as Lieutenant. Boatswain – no shoulder-bars; cap with two thin bands of gold lace, plain gold anchor badge. Master's Mate – as boatswain, but silver anchor on cap; single-breasted coat. Rated Masters' Mate – as Masters' Mate, but with double-breasted short jacket, no cap-lace.

Rank-markings after 1863 were as follows: Rear-Admiral: eight ¼-inch bands of lace on sleeves, gold star above top band; silver fouled anchor and two stars on shoulder-bars; cap-badge of two silver stars in wreath. Commodore – as Rear-Admiral, but seven laces on sleeve, silver star and gold fouled anchor on shoulder-bars, silver fouled anchor in cap-wreath. Captain – six sleeve-laces, silver eagle resting on anchor on shoulder-bars. Cap-badge as Commodore. Lieutenant-Commander – four sleeve-laces, silver fouled anchor and two gold oak-leaves on shoulder-bars; cap-badge as Commodore. Lieutenant – three sleeve-laces, silver fouled anchor and two gold bars on shoulder-bars; cap-badge as Commodore. Master – two sleeve-laces, shoulder-bars as Lieutenant but one gold bar, cap-badge as Commodore. Ensign – one sleeve-lace, silver fouled anchor on shoulder-bars, cap-badge as Commodore. Gunner – gold star on sleeve, plain gold lace shoulder-bars, no device within cap-wreath. Boatswain – as Gunner, but silver letter 'B' on shoulder-bars. Carpenter – as Gunner, but no badge on sleeve, letter 'C' on shoulder-bars. Sailmaker – as Gunner, but no sleeve-badge. Midshipman – as Gunner, no shoulder-bars. Masters' Mate – as Midshipman, but single-breasted coat.

The peaked undress cap was often replaced by the straw hat in summer; the frock-coat was often worn open to expose the waistcoat, white trousers being popular in summer. A shorter jacket was allowed for service dress.

Confederate naval dress for officers was of the same basic design as that of the Army, with steel-grey frock-coats, and bars of gold lace on the sleeves to indicate rank: Flag Officer four bars (the upper one looped), Captain three, Commander two, Lieutenant one, Master one without loop, Midshipman no lace, but three buttons on top of cuff. Waistcoat and trousers were white or steel-grey. Shoulder-bars were light blue, edged gold, bearing rank badges: Flag Officer four stars, Captain three, Commander two, Lieutenant one star, Master no star, Midshipman a strip of gold lace; Surgeons had black bars with one or two olive-sprigs in gold in the centre, Assistant-Surgeons the same but with gold olive-leaves; Paymaster as Surgeon but dark green bars, Assistant-Paymaster as Assistant-Surgeon, but dark green bars; Chief Engineer blue bars with gold live-oak sprigs in the centre.

Cap-badges were: Flag Officer – fouled anchor in oak-wreath, four stars above, all in gold, cap with gold lace band; Captain the same, but three stars; Commander two stars; Lieutenant one star; Master no star; Passed Midshipman just a fouled anchor; senior Surgeon three stars in olive-wreath, Surgeon with two stars, Assistant-Surgeon one, junior Assistant no star; Paymaster and Engineer ranks as Surgeon, with gold letter 'E' for Engineers. Straw hats and grey or white jackets could be worn on service.

cloth jackets and trousers or grey woollen 'frocks' with white duck collars and cuffs, black hats and black handkerchiefs; the rating illustrated, however, shows the dress common to both navies in action, allowing both comfort and freedom of movement. Confederate petty officers wore black 'fouled anchor' rank badges on the right or left sleeve depending on rank (as in the Federal Navy) (dark blue badges when white summer dress was worn). In both navies, chief petty officers wore jackets like those of the junior commissioned ranks. Crews of Confederate privateers were officially civilians, only the officers having Confederate commissions; they therefore wore ordinary civilian dress.

The U.S. Petty Officer is shown in white 'summer rig'; the rank-badge was worn on the left-hand sleeve by lower ranks and the right-hand sleeve by Boatswain's Mates and higher. In ordinary dress, the uniform was similar in cut, but in dark blue. The 'sailor collar' of the blouse bore a small star badge in the rear corners. The Petty Officer is shown armed with a heavy-bladed naval cutlass, together with a 'Navy' pistol. Frequently, combinations of 'blues' and 'whites' were worn in the same uniform, usually at the commanding officer's discretion.

64. a) Seaman,
   Confederate Navy.
   b) Petty Officer,
   U.S. Navy, Summer Dress.
Confederate seamen wore grey

184

ORDERS OF BATTLE – GETTYSBURG

NOTE – abbreviations used below:
Bde: Brigade
B.Gen.: Brigadier-General
M.Gen.: Major-General
Lt.Gen.: Lieutenant-General

Army of the Potomac (M.Gen. G. G. Meade)

1st CORPS (M.GEN. J. F. REYNOLDS)
1st Division (B.Gen. J. S. Wadsworth)
    1st Bde (B.Gen. S. Meredith) – 2nd, 6th and 7th Wis.; 19th Ind.;
    24th Mich.
    2nd Bde (B.Gen. L. Cutler) – 14th, 47th, 76th and 95th N.Y.; 7th
    Ind.
2nd Division (B.Gen. J. Robinson)
    1st Bde (B.Gen. G. R. Paul) – 94th and 104th N.Y.; 11th and
    107th Pa.; 16th Maine; 13th Mass.
    2nd Bde (B.Gen. H. Baxter) – 83rd and 97th N.Y.; 19th and 88th
    Pa.; 12th Mass.
3rd Division (M.Gen. A. Doubleday)
    1st Bde (B.Gen. T. Rowley) – 20th N.Y.; 121st, 142nd and 151st
    Pa.
    2nd Bde (Col. R. Stone) – 143rd, 149th and 150th Pa.
    3rd Bde (B.Gen. G. Stannard) – 12th, 13th, 14th, 15th and 16th
    Vt.
Artillery Bde (Col. C. Wainwright) – 2nd and 5th Maine; 'B' 1st Pa;
    'B' 4th U.S.; 'L' 1st N.Y.

2nd CORPS (M.GEN. W. S. HANCOCK)
1st Division (B.Gen. J. C. Caldwell)
    1st Bde (Col. E. E. Cross) – 81st and 148th Pa.; 5th N.H.; 61st
    N.Y.
    2nd Bde (Col. P. Kelly) – 63rd, 69th and 116th N.Y.; 116th Pa.;
    28th Mass.
    3rd Bde (B.Gen. S. K. Zook) – 52nd, 57th and 66th N.Y.; 140th
    Pa.

4th Bde (Col. J. R. Brook) – 53rd and 145th Pa.; 27th Conn.; 64th N.Y.; 2nd Del.

2nd Division (B.Gen. J. Gibbon)

1st Bde (B.Gen. W. Harrow) – 19th Maine; 15th Mass.; 82nd N.Y.; 1st Minn.

2nd Bde (B.Gen. A. S. Webb) – 69th, 71st, 72nd and 106th Pa.

3rd Bde (Col. N. J. Hall) – 19th and 20th Mass.; 42nd and 59th N.Y.; 7th Mich.

3rd Division (B.Gen. A. Hays)

1st Bde (Col. S. S. Carroll) – 4th and 8th Ohio; 14th Ind.; 7th W.Va.

2nd Bde (Col. T. A. Smyth) – 14th Conn.; 108th N.Y.; 12th N.J.; 1st Del.

3rd Bde (Col. G. Willard) – 39th, 111th, 125th and 126th N.Y.

Artillery Bde (Capt. J. G. Hazard) – 'A' and 'B' 1st R.I.; 'A' and 'I' 1st U.S.; 'B' 1st N.Y.

Cavalry Squadron (Capt. R. Johnson) – 'D' and 'K' 6th N.Y.

3rd CORPS (M.GEN. D. E. SICKLES)

1st Division (M.Gen. D. B. Birney)

1st Bde (B.Gen. C. Graham) – 63rd, 68th, 105th, 114th and 141st Pa.

2nd Bde (B.Gen. J. H. Ward) – 3rd and 4th Maine; 86th and 124th N.Y.; 20th Ind.; 99th Pa.; 1st and 2nd U.S. Sharpshooters.

3rd Bde (Col. P. R. de Trobriand) – 3rd and 5th Mich.; 17th Maine; 40th N.Y.; 110th Pa.

2nd Division (B.Gen. A. Humphreys)

1st Bde (B.Gen. J. B. Carr) – 1st, 11th and 16th Mass.; 26th and 84th Pa.; 11th N.J.; 12th N.H.

2nd Bde (Col. W. Brewster) – 70th, 71st, 72nd, 73rd, 74th and 120th N.Y.

3rd Bde (Col. G. C. Burling) – 5th, 6th, 7th and 8th N.J.; 115th Pa.; 2nd N.H.

Artillery Bde (Capt. G. Randolph) – 'B' and 'D' 1st N.J.; 'E' 1st R.I.; 'K' 4th U.S.; 'D' 1st N.Y.; 4th N.Y.

5th CORPS (M.GEN. G. SYKES)

1st Division (B.Gen. J. Barnes)

1st Bde (Col. W. S. Tilton) – 18th and 22nd Mass.; 1st Mich.; 118th Pa.

2nd Bde (Col. J. B. Sweitzer) – 9th and 32nd Mass.; 4th Mich.; 62nd Pa.

3rd Bde (Col. S. Vincent) – 20th Maine; 44th N.Y.; 83rd Pa.; 16th Mich.

2nd Division (B.Gen. R. B. Ayres)

1st Bde (Col. H. Day) – 3rd, 4th, 6th, 12th and 14th U.S. Infantry.

2nd Bde (Col. S. Burbank) – 2nd, 7th, 10th, 11th and 17th U.S. Infantry.

3rd Bde (B.Gen. S. H. Weed) – 140th and 146th N.Y.; 91st and 155th Pa.

3rd Division (B.Gen. S. Crawford)

1st Bde (Col. W. McCandless) – 1st, 2nd, 6th, 11th and 13th Pa. Reserves.

2nd Bde (Col. J. W. Fisher) – 5th, 9th, 10th and 12th Pa. Reserves.

Artillery Bde (Capt. A. P. Martin) – 'D' and 'I' 5th U.S.; 'C' 1st N.Y.; 'L' 1st Ohio; 'C' Mass.

Provost Guard (Capt. H. W. Ryder) – 'E' and 'D' 12th N.Y.

6th CORPS (M.GEN. J. SEDGEWICK)

1st Division (B.Gen. H. G. Wright)

1st Bde (B.Gen. A. Torbert) – 1st, 2nd, 3rd and 15th N.J.

2nd Bde (B.Gen. J. Bartlett) – 95th and 96th Pa.; 5th Maine; 121st N.Y.

3rd Bde (B.Gen. D. Russell) – 49th and 119th Pa.; 6th Maine; 5th Wis.

2nd Division (B.Gen. A. P. Howe)

2nd Bde (Col. L. A. Grant) – 3rd, 4th, 5th and 6th Vermont.

3rd Bde (B.Gen. T. Neill) – 43rd, 49th and 77th N.Y.; 61st Pa.; 7th Maine.

3rd Division (B.Gen. F. Wheaton)

1st Bde (B.Gen. A. Shaler) – 65th, 67th and 122nd N.Y.; 23rd and 82nd Pa.

2nd Bde (Col. H. L. Eustis) – 7th, 10th and 37th Mass.; 2nd R.I.

3rd Bde (Col. D. I. Nevin) – 93rd, 98th, 102nd and 139th Pa.; 62nd N.Y.

Artillery Bde (Col. C. H. Tompkins) – 'D' and 'G' 2nd U.S.; 'C' and 'G' 1st R.I.; 1st and 3rd N.Y.; 'A' 1st Mass.; 'F' 5th U.S.

Cavalry detachment (Capt. W. L. Craft) – 'H' 1st Pa.; 'L' 1st N.J.

11th CORPS (M.GEN. O. O. HOWARD)
1st Division (B.Gen. F. C. Barlow)
    1st Bde (Col. L. von Gilsa) – 41st, 54th and 69th N.Y.; 153rd Pa.
    2nd Bde (B.Gen. A. Ames) – 25th, 75th and 107th Ohio; 17th Conn.
2nd Division (B.Gen. A. von Steinwehr)
    1st Bde (Col. C. R. Coster) – 27th and 73rd Pa.; 134th and 154th N.Y.
    2nd Bde (Col. O. Smith) – 55th and 73rd Ohio; 3rd Mass.; 136th N.Y.
3rd Division (M.Gen. C. Schurz)
    1st Bde (B.Gen. von Schimmelpfennig) – 45th and 157th N.Y.; 74th Pa.; 61st Ohio; 82nd Ill.
    2nd Bde (Col. W. Kryzanowski) – 58th and 119th N.Y.; 75th Pa.; 82nd Ohio; 26th Wis.
Artillery Bde (Maj. T. W. Osborne) – 'I' and 'K' 1st Ohio; 'I' 1st N.Y.; 'G' 4th U.S.; 13th N.Y.

12th CORPS (M.GEN. H. W. SLOCUM)
1st Division (B.Gen. T. H. Ruger)
    1st Bde (Col. A. McDougall) – 5th and 20th Conn.; 123rd and 145th N.Y.; 46th Pa.; 3rd Maryland.
    2nd Bde (B.Gen. H. Lockwood) – 150th N.Y.; 1st Maryland.
    3rd Bde (Col. S. Colgrove) – 2nd Mass.; 107th N.Y.; 13th N.J.; 27th Ind.; 3rd Wis.
2nd Division (B.Gen. J. Geary)
    1st Bde (Col. C. Candy) – 5th, 7th, 29th and 66th Ohio; 28th and 147th Pa.
    2nd Bde (Col. G. A. Cobham) – 29th, 109th and 111th Pa.
    3rd Bde (B.Gen. G. S. Green) – 60th, 78th, 102nd, 137th and 149th N.Y.
Artillery Bde (Lt. E. D. Muhlenberg) – 'F' 4th U.S.; 'K' 5th U.S.; 'M' 1st N.Y.; Knap's Pa. Bty.
Headquarter Guard – Btn. 10th Maine.

CAVALRY CORPS (M.GEN. A. PLEASONTON)
1st Division (B.Gen. J. Buford)
    1st Bde (Col. W. Gamble) – 8th N.Y.; 8th Ill.; 2 sqdns. 12th Ill.; 3 sqdns. 3rd Ill.
    2nd Bde (Col. T. Devin) – 6th and 9th N.Y.; 17th Pa.

Reserve Bde (B.Gen. W. Merritt) – 1st, 2nd, 5th and 6th U.S.; 6th Pa.

2nd Division (B.Gen. D. M. Gregg)

1st Bde (Col. J. B. McIntosh) – 1st and 3rd Pa.; 1st Maryland; 1st Mass.

2nd Bde (Col. P. Huey) – 2nd and 4th N.Y.; 8th Pa.; 6th Ohio.

3rd Bde (Col. J. I. Gregg) – 4th and 16th Pa.; 10th N.Y.; 1st Maine.

3rd Division (B.Gen. J. Kilpatrick)

1st Bde (B.Gen. E. Farnsworth) – 5th N.Y.; 18th Pa.; 1st Vt.; 1st W.Va.

2nd Bde (B.Gen. G. A. Custer) – 1st, 5th, 6th and 7th Mich.

HORSE ARTILLERY

1st Bde (Capt. J. M. Robertson) – 'B', 'L' and 'M' 2nd U.S.; 'C' 3rd U.S.; 'E' 4th U.S.; 6th N.Y.; 9th Mich.

2nd Bde (Capt. J. C. Tidball) – 'G', 'E' and 'K' 1st U.S.; 'A' and 'K' 2nd U.S.; 'C' 3rd U.S.

ARTILLERY RESERVE (B.GEN. R. O. TYLER)

1st Regular Bde (Capt. D. Ransom) – 'H' 1st U.S.; 'F' and 'K' 3rd U.S.; 'C' 4th U.S.; 'C' 5th U.S.

1st Volunteer Bde (Lt.Col. McGilvery) – 5th and 9th Mass.; 15th N.Y.; Pa. Indepen. Bty.

2nd Volunteer Bde (Capt. E. D. Taft) – 'B' and 'M' 1st Conn.; 2nd Conn.; 5th N.Y.

3rd Volunteer Bde (Capt. Huntington) – 'F' and 'G' 1st Pa.; 'H' 1st Ohio; 'A' 1st N.H.; 'C' 1st W.Va.

4th Volunteer Bde (Capt. Fitzhugh) – 'B', 'G' and 'K' 1st N.Y.; 'A' 1st Maryland; 6th Maine, 'A' 1st N.J.

Army of Northern Virginia (Gen. R. E. Lee)

1st CORPS (LT.GEN. J. LONGSTREET)

M.Gen. L. McLaws' Division

Kershaw's Bde – 2nd, 3rd, 7th, 8th and 15th S.C.; 3rd S.C. Btn.

Semmes' Bde – 2nd, 15th, 17th and 20th Ga.

Barksdale's Bde – 13th, 17th, 18th and 21st Miss.

Wofford's Bde – 16th, 18th and 24th Ga.; Phillips' Ga. Legion; Cobb's Ga. Legion.

M.Gen. G. E. Pickett's Division
    Garnett's Bde – 8th, 18th, 19th, 28th and 56th Va.
    Armistead's Bde – 9th, 14th, 38th, 53rd and 57th Va.
    Kemper's Bde – 1st, 3rd, 7th, 11th and 24th Va.
M.Gen. J. B. Hood's Division
    Law's Bde – 4th, 15th, 44th, 47th and 48th Ala.
    Anderson's Bde – 7th, 8th, 9th and 11th Ga.; 10th Ga. Btn.
    Robertson's Bde – 1st, 4th and 5th Texas; 3rd Ark.
    Benning's Bde – 10th, 50th, 51st and 53rd Ga.
Artillery (Col. J. B. Walton)
    Cabell's Btn – McCarty's, Manly's, Carlton's and Fraser's Btys.
    Dearing's Btn – Macon's, Blount's, Stribling's and Caskie's Btys.
    Henry's Btn – Beachman's, Reilly's, Latham's, and Gordon's Btys.
    Alexander's Btn – Jordan's, Rhett's, Moody's, Parker's and
        Taylor's Btys.
    Eshleman's Btn – Squire's, Miller's, Richardson's and Norcom's
        Btys.

2nd CORPS (LT.GEN. R. S. EWELL)
M.Gen. J. A. Early's Division
    Hay's Bde – 5th, 6th, 8th, 9th and 17th La.
    Gordon's Bde – 13th, 26th, 31st, 38th, 60th and 61st Ga.
    Hoke's Bde (Avery commanding) – 5th, 21st, 54th and 57th N.C.;
        1st N.C. Btn.
    Smith's Bde – 13th, 31st, 49th, 52nd and 58th Va.
M.Gen. E. Johnson's Division
    Steuart's Bde – 10th, 23rd and 27th Va.; 1st and 3rd N.C.
    Walker's (Stonewall) Brigade – 2nd, 4th, 5th, 27th and 33rd Va.
    Nicholl's Bde – 1st, 2nd, 10th, 14th and 15th La.
    Jones' Bde – 21st, 42nd, 44th, 48th and 50th Va.
M.Gen. R. E. Rodes' Division
    Daniel's Bde – 32nd, 43rd, 54th and 53rd N.C.; 2nd N.C. Btn.
    Doles' Bde – 4th, 12th, 21st and 44th Ga.
    Iverson's Bde – 5th, 12th, 20th and 23rd N.C.
    Ramseur's Bde – 2nd, 4th, 14th and 30th N.C.
    Rodes' Bde (O'Neal commanding) – 3rd, 5th, 6th, 12th and 26th Ala.
Artillery (Col. S. Crutchfield)
    Braxton's Btn – Page's, Fry's, Carter's and Reese's Btys.
    Jones' Btn – Carrington's, Garber's, Thompson's and Tanner's
        Btys.

Andrew's Btn – Brown's, Dermot's, Carpenter's and Raine's Btys.
Brown's Btn – Dauce's, Watson's, Smith's, Huff's and Grahams' Btys.

3rd CORPS (LT.GEN. A. P. HILL)

M.Gen. R. H. Anderson's Division
   Wilcox's Bde – 8th, 9th, 10th, 11th and 14th Ala.
   Mahone's Bde – 6th, 12th, 16th, 41st and 61st Va.
   Posey's Bde – 12th, 16th, 19th and 46th Miss.
   Wright's Bde – 2nd, 3rd, 22nd and 48th Ga.
   Perry's Bde – 2nd, 5th and 8th Fla.
M.Gen. H. Heth's Division
   Pettigrew's Bde – 11th, 17th, 26th, 42nd, 44th, 47th and 52nd N.C.
   Brockenbrough's Bde – 40th, 47th and 55th Va.
   Archer's Bde – 1st, 7th and 14th Tenna.; 13th Ala.
   Davis' Bde – 2nd, 11th and 42nd Miss.; 55th N.C.
M.Gen. W. D. Pender's Division
   McGowan's Bde – 1st, 12th, 13th and 14th N.C.
   Lane's Bde – 7th, 18th, 28th, 33rd and 37th Va.
   Thomas' Bde – 14th, 35th, 45th and 49th Ga.
   Scales' Bde – 13th, 16th, 22nd, 34th and 38th N.C.
Artillery (Col. R. L. Walker)
   McIntosh's Btn – Hurt's, Rice's, Luck's and Johnson's Btys.
   Garnett's Btn – Lewis', Maurin's, Moore's and Grandy's Btys.
   Cutshaw's Btn – Wyatt's, Woolfolk's and Brooke's Btys.
   Pegram's Btn – Brunson's, Davidson's, Crenshaw's, McGraw's and Marye's Btys.
   Cutts' Btn (Lane commanding) – Wingfield's, Ross' and Patterson's Btys.

CAVALRY CORPS (LT.GEN. J. E. B. STUART)
B.Gen. W. Hampton's Bde.
B.Gen. F. Lee's Bde.
B.Gen. W. H. F. Lee's Bde. (Col. Chambliss commanding)
B.Gen. B. H. Robertson's Bde.
B.Gen. W. E. Jones' Bde.
B.Gen. J. D. Imboden's Bde.
B.Gen. A. G. Jenkin's Bde.

Fig. 1. Regulation 'C.S.A.'
(Confederate States of America)
plate.

Fig. 2. Plate with a design
based upon the 'Southern Cross'
battle-flag.

Fig. 3. Elaborate, unofficially-
issued 'Texas Star' design.

Fig. 4. North Carolina state
plate.

Fig. 5. Virginia state plate.

Fig. 6. Virginia state plate.

CONFEDERATE ARMY BELT PLATES.